Teach Yourself
VISUALLY™
Photoshop® 7

by Mike Wooldridge

Visual™

From
maranGraphics®

&

Wiley Publishing, Inc.

Teach Yourself VISUALLY™ Photoshop® 7

Published by
Wiley Publishing, Inc.
909 Third Avenue
New York, NY 10022

Published simultaneously in Canada

Copyright © 2002 by Wiley Publishing, Inc., Indianapolis, Indiana

Certain designs and illustrations Copyright © 1992-2002 maranGraphics, Inc., used with maranGraphics' permission.

maranGraphics, Inc.
5755 Coopers Avenue
Mississauga, Ontario, Canada
L4Z 1R9

Library of Congress Control Number: 2002102422

ISBN: 0-7645-3682-6

Manufactured in the United States of America

10 9 8 7 6 5 4 3

1K/RX/QW/QS/IN

Trademark Acknowledgments

Important Numbers

For U.S. corporate orders, please call maranGraphics at 800-469-6616 or fax 905-890-9434.

For general information on our other products and services or to obtain technical support please contact our Customer Care Department within the U.S. at 800-762-2974, outside the U.S. at 317-572-3993 or fax 317-572-4002.

Permissions

Wiley Publishing, Inc. is a trademark of Wiley Publishing, Inc.

U.S. Corporate Sales	**U.S. Trade Sales**
Contact maranGraphics at (800) 469-6616 or Fax (905) 890-9434.	Contact Wiley at (800) 762-2974 or fax (317) 572-4002.

Some comments from our readers...

"I have to praise you and your company on the fine products you turn out. I have twelve of the *Teach Yourself VISUALLY* and *Simplified* books in my house. They were instrumental in helping me pass a difficult computer course. Thank you for creating books that are easy to follow."

  —*Gordon Justin (Brielle, NJ)*

"I commend your efforts and your success. I teach in an outreach program for the Dr. Eugene Clark Library in Lockhart, TX. Your *Teach Yourself VISUALLY* books are incredible and I use them in my computer classes. All my students love them!"

  —*Michele Schalin (Lockhart, TX)*

"Thank you so much for helping people like me learn about computers. The Maran family is just what the doctor ordered. Thank you, thank you, thank you."

  —*Carol Moten (New Kensington, PA)*

"I would like to take this time to compliment maranGraphics on creating such great books. Thank you for making it clear. Keep up the good work."

  —*Kirk Santoro (Burbank, CA)*

"I write to extend my thanks and appreciation for your books. They are clear, easy to follow, and straight to the point. Keep up the good work!"

  —*Seward Kollie (Dakar, Senegal)*

"What fantastic teaching books you have produced! Congratulations to you and your staff. You deserve the Nobel prize in Education in the Software category. Thanks for helping me to understand computers."

  —*Bruno Tonon (Melbourne, Australia)*

"Over time, I have bought a number of your 'Read Less – Learn More' books. For me, they are THE way to learn anything easily."

  —*José A. Mazón (Cuba, NY)*

"I was introduced to maranGraphics about four years ago and YOU ARE THE GREATEST THING THAT EVER HAPPENED TO INTRODUCTORY COMPUTER BOOKS!"

  —*Glenn Nettleton (Huntsville, AL)*

"Compliments To The Chef!! Your books are extraordinary! Or, simply put, Extra-Ordinary, meaning way above the rest! THANK YOU THANK YOU THANK YOU! for creating these."

  —*Christine J. Manfrin (Castle Rock, CO)*

"I'm a grandma who was pushed by an 11-year-old grandson to join the computer age. I found myself hopelessly confused and frustrated until I discovered the Visual series. I'm no expert by any means now, but I'm a lot further along than I would have been otherwise. Thank you!"

  —*Carol Louthain (Logansport, IN)*

"Thank you, thank you, thank you....for making it so easy for me to break into this high-tech world. I now own four of your books. I recommend them to anyone who is a beginner like myself. Now....if you could just do one for programming VCRs, it would make my day!"

  —*Gay O'Donnell (Calgary, Alberta, Canada)*

"You're marvelous! I am greatly in your debt."

  —*Patrick Baird (Lacey, WA)*

**maranGraphics is a family-run business
located near Toronto, Canada.**

At **maranGraphics**, we believe in producing great computer books — one book at a time.

maranGraphics has been producing high-technology products for over 25 years, which enables us to offer the computer book community a unique communication process.

Our computer books use an integrated communication process, which is very different from the approach used in other computer books. Each spread is, in essence, a flow chart — the text and screen shots are totally incorporated into the layout of the spread.

Introductory text and helpful tips complete the learning experience.

maranGraphics' approach encourages the left and right sides of the brain to work together — resulting in faster orientation and greater memory retention.

Above all, we are very proud of the handcrafted nature of our books. Our carefully-chosen writers are experts in their fields, and spend countless hours researching and organizing the content for each topic. Our artists rebuild every screen shot to provide the best

clarity possible, making our screen shots the most precise and easiest to read in the industry. We strive for perfection, and believe that the time spent handcrafting each element results in the best computer books money can buy.

Thank you for purchasing this book. We hope you enjoy it!

Sincerely,

Robert Maran
President
maranGraphics
Rob@maran.com
www.maran.com

CREDITS

Acquisitions, Editorial, and Media Development

Editorial Manager
Rev Mengle

Acquisitions Editor
Jen Dorsey

Product Development Supervisor
Lindsay Sandman

Project Editor
Sarah Hellert

Technical Editor
Dennis Cohen

Permissions Editor
Laura Moss

Copy Editor
Jill Mazurcyk

Special Help
Mac OS X material provided by Dennis Cohen,
co-author of *Macworld Mac OS X Bible* and
technical editor of this book.

Production

Book Design
maranGraphics®

Production Coordinator
Dale White

Layout
Melanie DesJardins, LeAndra Johnson,
Kristin McMullan, Heather Pope

Screen Artists
Mark Harris, Jill A. Proll

Illustrators
Ronda David-Burroughs, David E. Gregory

Proofreader
Laura Albert, Susan Moritz

Quality Control
John Bitter, Carl Pierce

Indexer
Anne Leach

Manufacturing
Allan Conley, Linda Cook,
Paul Gilchrist, Jennifer Guynn

ACKNOWLEDGMENTS

General and Administrative

Wiley Technology Publishing Group: Richard Swadley, Vice President and Executive Group Publisher;
Bob Ipsen, Vice President and Executive Publisher; Barry Pruett, Vice President and Publisher; Joseph Wikert,
Vice President and Publisher; Mary Bednarek, Editorial Director; Mary C. Corder, Editorial Director;
Andy Cummings, Editorial Director.
Wiley Production for Branded Press: Debbie Stailey, Production Director

ABOUT THE AUTHOR

Mike Wooldridge is a Web developer in the San Francisco Bay Area. He has authored several other Visual books, including Teach Yourself Visually Photoshop 6, Teach Yourself Visually Photoshop Elements, and Teach Yourself Visually Dreamweaver 4. His Web site is at www.mediacosm.com.

AUTHOR'S ACKNOWLEDGMENTS

Thanks to Project Editor Sarah Hellert and everyone else at Wiley Publishing who worked on this book.

To Griffin, my three-year-old son who
likes to tap on my keyboard
and close my applications.

TABLE OF CONTENTS

Chapter 1

Chapter 2

Chapter 3

Chapter 4

MAKING SELECTIONS

Chapter 5

MANIPULATING SELECTIONS

Chapter 6

SPECIFYING COLOR MODES

TABLE OF CONTENTS

Chapter 7

PAINTING AND DRAWING WITH COLOR

Chapter 8

ADJUSTING COLORS

Chapter 9

WORKING WITH LAYERS

Chapter 10

APPLYING LAYER EFFECTS

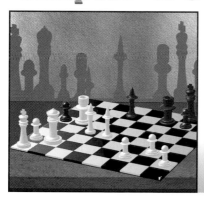

TABLE OF CONTENTS

Chapter 11

Chapter 12

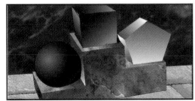

Chapter 13

Chapter 14

AUTOMATING YOUR WORK

Chapter 15

SAVING IMAGES

Chapter 16

PRINTING IMAGES

Chapter 17

PERFORMANCE TIPS

CHAPTER 1

Getting Started

Are you interested in creating, modifying, combining, and optimizing digital images on your computer? This chapter introduces you to Adobe Photoshop, a popular software application for working with digital images.

WORK WITH IMAGES

Photoshop lets you create, modify, combine, and optimize digital images. You can then save the images to print out or use online.

Manipulate Photos

As its name suggests, Photoshop excels at editing digital photographs. You can use the program to make subtle changes, such as to adjust the color in a scanned photo, or you can use its elaborate filters to make your snapshots look like abstract art. See Chapter 8 for more about adjusting color and Chapter 11 for more about filters.

Paint Pictures

Photoshop's painting features make it a formidable illustration tool as well as a photo editor. You can apply colors or patterns to your images with a variety of brush styles. See Chapter 7 for more about applying color. In addition, you can use the program's typographic tools to integrate stylized letters and words into your images. See Chapter 13 for more about type.

Create a Digital Collage

You can combine different image elements in Photoshop. Your compositions can include photos, scanned art, text, and anything else you can save on your computer as a digital image. By placing elements in Photoshop onto separate layers, you can move, transform, and customize them independently of one another. See Chapter 9 for more about layers.

Organize Your Photos

Photoshop offers useful ways to keep your images organized after you have edited them. You can archive your images on contact sheets or display them in a Web photo gallery.

Put Your Images to Work

After you edit your work, you can utilize your images in a variety of ways. Photoshop lets you print your images, save them in a format suitable for placement on a Web page, or prepare them for use in a page-layout program. See Chapter 16 for more about printing. See Chapter 15 for more about using images on the Web.

UNDERSTANDING PHOTOSHOP

Photoshop's tools let you move, color, stylize, and add text to your images. You can optimize photographs, or turn them into interesting works of art.

Understanding Pixels

Digital images in Photoshop consist of tiny, solid-color squares called pixels. Photoshop works its magic by rearranging and recoloring these squares. If you zoom in close, you can see the pixels that make up your image. For more on the Zoom tool, see Chapter 2.

Choose Your Pixels

To edit specific pixels in your image, you first have to select them by using one of Photoshop's selection tools. See Chapter 4 for more on selection tools. Photoshop also has a number of commands that help you select specific parts of your image, including commands that expand or contract your existing selection or select pixels of a specific color.

Paint

After selecting your pixels, you can apply color to them by using Photoshop's paintbrush, airbrush, and pencil tools. You can also fill your selections with solid or semitransparent colors, patterns, or pixels copied from another part of your image. Painting is covered in Chapter 7.

Adjust Color

You can brighten, darken, and change the hue of colors in parts of your image with Photoshop's Dodge, Burn, and similar tools. Other commands display interactive dialog boxes that let you make wholesale color adjustments, letting you precisely correct overly dark or light digital photographs. See Chapter 8 for details.

Apply Effects and Filters

Photoshop's effects let you easily add drop shadows, frame borders, and other styles to your images. You can also perform complex color manipulations or distortions by using filters. Filters can make your image look like an impressionist painting, apply sharpening or blurring, or distort your image in various ways. Chapters 10 and 11 cover effects and filters.

Add Type

Photoshop's type tools enable you to easily apply titles and labels to your images. You can combine these tools with the program's special effects commands to create warped, 3D, or wildly colored type. You can find out more about type in Chapter 13.

START PHOTOSHOP ON A PC

You can start Photoshop
on a PC and begin
creating and editing
digital images.

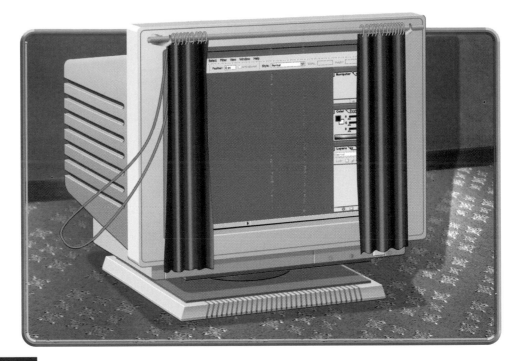

START PHOTOSHOP ON A PC

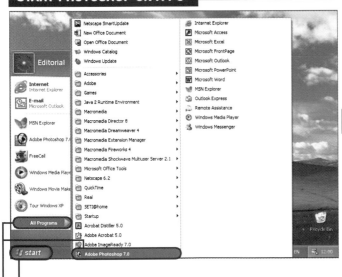

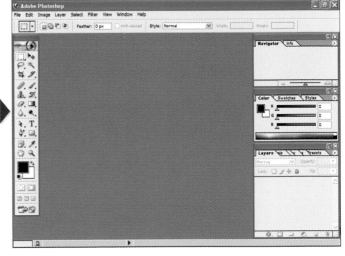

1 Click **Start**.

2 Click **All Programs**.

3 Click **Adobe
Photoshop 7.0**.

*Note: Your path to the Photoshop
program may be different, depending
on how you installed your software.*

■ Photoshop starts.

START PHOTOSHOP ON A MAC

You can start Photoshop on a Macintosh and begin creating and editing digital images.

START PHOTOSHOP ON A MAC

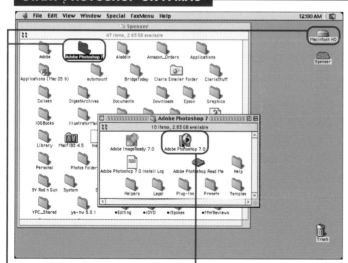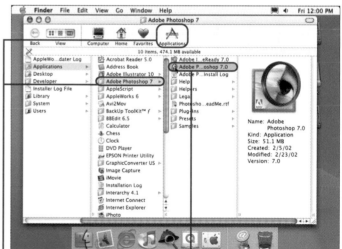

START PHOTOSHOP WITH MAC OS 9

1 Double-click your hard drive.

2 Double-click the Adobe Photoshop 7 folder (📁).

3 Double-click the Adobe Photoshop 7.0 icon (🔵).

Note: The exact location of the Adobe Photoshop icon may be different, depending on how you installed your software.

■ Photoshop starts.

START PHOTOSHOP WITH MAC OS X

1 Click the Applications button (🅰).

2 Click the Adobe Photoshop 7 folder (📁).

3 Double-click the Adobe Photoshop 7.0 icon (🔵).

Note: The exact location of the Adobe Photoshop icon may be different, depending on how you installed your software.

■ Photoshop starts.

THE PHOTOSHOP WORKSPACE

You can use a combination of tools, menu commands, and palette-based features to open and edit your digital images in Photoshop.

Menu Bar

Displays the menus that contain most of Photoshop's commands.

Options Bar

Displays controls that let you customize the selected tool in the toolbox.

Toolbox

Displays a variety of icons, each one representing an image-editing tool. You click and drag inside your image to apply most of the tools.

Image Window

Contains each image you open in Photoshop.

Palettes

Small, free-floating windows that give you access to common commands and resources.

You can get raw material for using Photoshop from a variety of sources.

Start from Scratch

You can create your Photoshop image from scratch by opening a blank canvas in the image window. Then you can apply color and patterns with Photoshop's painting tools or cut and paste parts of other images to create a composite. See the section "Create a New Image" for more on opening a blank canvas.

Scanned Photos and Art

A scanner gives you an inexpensive way to convert existing paper-based content into digital form. You can scan photos and art into your computer, retouch and stylize them in Photoshop, and then output them to a color printer.

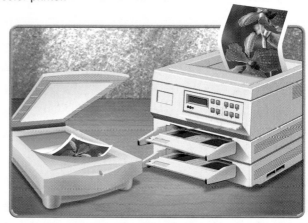

Clip Art

If you want a wide variety of image content to work with, consider buying a clip art collection. Such collections usually include illustrations, photos, and decorative icons that you can use in imaging projects. Most software stores sell clip art; you can also buy downloadable clip art online.

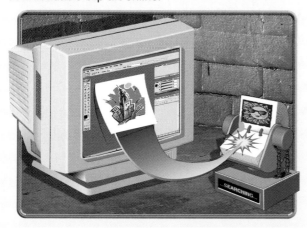

Digital Photos

Digital cameras are a great way to get digital images onto your computer. Most digital cameras save their images in JPEG or TIFF format, both of which you can open and edit in Photoshop. The program's color adjustment tools are great for correcting color and exposure flaws in digital camera images.

SET PREFERENCES

Photoshop's Preferences dialog boxes let you change default settings and customize how the program looks.

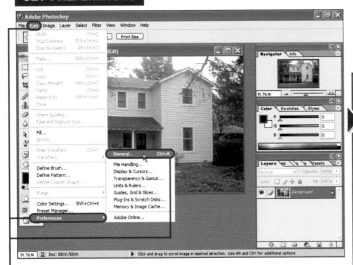

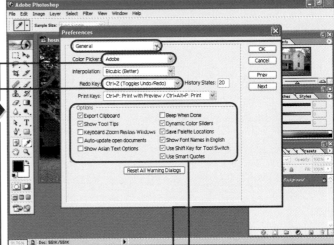

1 Access the Preferences menu.

■ In Windows and Mac OS 9, click **Edit**, then **Preferences**, and then **General**.

■ In Mac OS X, click **Photoshop**, then **Preferences**, and then **General**.

■ The Preferences dialog box appears and displays General options.

2 Click here to determine which dialog box appears when you select a color.

3 Click here to select a keyboard shortcut for redoing a command.

4 Click the interface options you want to use (☐ changes to ☑).

5 Click ☑ (⬍) and select **Display & Cursors**.

What type of measurement units should I use in Photoshop?

Typically, you should use the units most applicable to the type of output you intend to use. Pixel units are useful for Web imaging because monitor dimensions are measured in pixels. Inches, centimeters, or picas are useful for print because those are standards for working on paper.

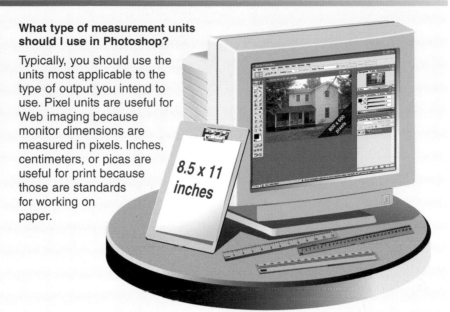

8.5 x 11 inches

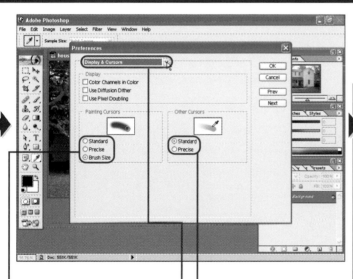

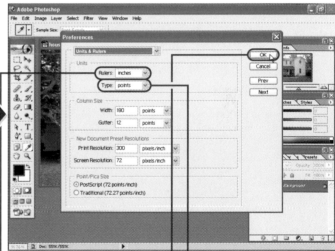

■ The Display & Cursors Preferences options appear.

6 Click a cursor type to use for the painting tools — the paintbrush, eraser, and others (○ changes to ⊙).

7 Click a cursor type to use for the other tools (○ changes to ⊙).

8 Click ⌄ (⬍) and select **Units & Rulers**.

■ The Units & Rulers Preferences options appear.

9 Click here to select the units for the window rulers. These units become the default units selected when you resize an image.

10 Click here to select the default units for type.

11 Click **OK**.

■ Photoshop sets preferences to your specifications.

Photoshop comes with plenty of electronic documentation that you can access in case you ever need help.

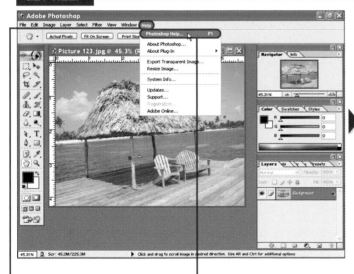

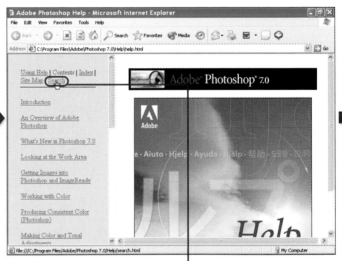

1 Click **Help**.

2 Click **Photoshop Help**.

■ Photoshop opens your default Web browser and displays the Help interface.

3 Click **Search** to search for information about a particular topic.

**How can I find details about my
Photoshop software?**

Click **Help** and then **System
Info**. A window opens
displaying information about
your Photoshop software,
including where it is
installed and what plug-
ins you have available. It
also lists basic information
about your computer's
operating system and
memory.

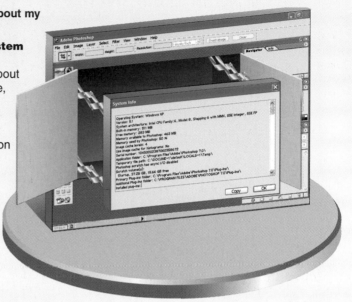

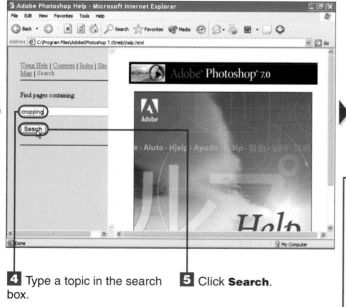

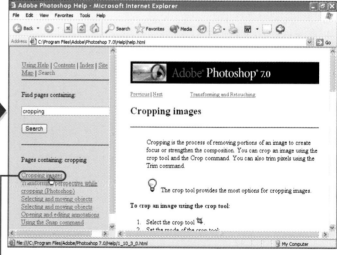

4 Type a topic in the search
box.

5 Click **Search**.

■ Relevant topics display in
the bottom left.

6 Click a topic.

■ Information about the
topic appears on the right.

OPEN AN IMAGE

You can open an existing image file in Photoshop to modify it or use it in a project.

Photoshop can open most image file formats: BMP, the standard Windows image format; PICT, the standard Macintosh image format; TIFF, a popular format for print on Windows and Macintosh; EPS, another print-oriented format; JPEG, a format for Web images; GIF, another format for Web images; PSD, Photoshop's native file format; and PDF, a popular format for creating illustrated text documents.

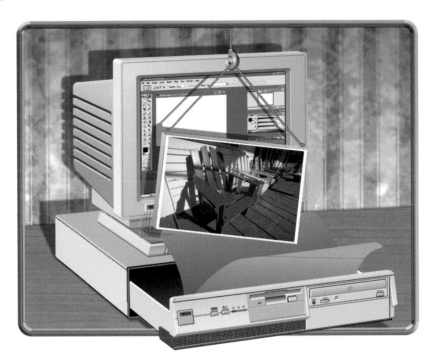

OPEN AN IMAGE

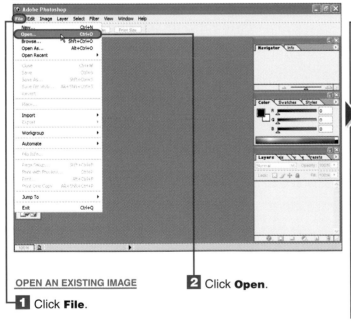

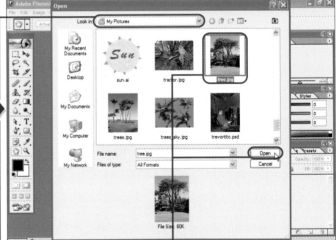

OPEN AN EXISTING IMAGE

1 Click **File**.

2 Click **Open**.

■ The Open dialog box appears.

3 Click here to browse to the folder that contains the image you want to open.

4 Click the filename of the image you want to open.

5 Click **Open**.

How do I open an image in Photoshop in Mac OS 9 or Mac OS X?

Mac OS 9 and Mac OS X have their own Open dialog boxes, extended with the additional Photoshop-specific controls. In either case, when you have navigated to the image you desire, you either double-click the image's name or icon or click the image's name or icon and then click Open, or press **Return** .

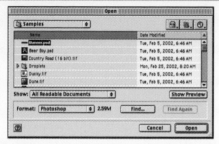

Mac OS 9

You can navigate to the folder containing the image you desire using the unlabelled popup menu at the top of the dialog box and the list area in the center of the dialog box.

Mac OS X

You can navigate to recently used and favorite folders using the From 🔽, or by using the Finder-like column view in the center of the dialog box.

■ Photoshop opens the image in a new window.

■ The filename appears in the title bar.

**OPEN RECENTLY
ACCESSED IMAGES**

1 Click **File**.

2 Click **Open Recent**.

■ A list of recently opened files displays.

Note: To specify the number of files that appear in the menu, see "Set Preferences."

3 Click the image's filename.

■ Photoshop opens the image in a new window.

BROWSE FOR AN IMAGE

You can open an existing image file by using Photoshop's File Browser. Browsing offers a user-friendly way to find and open your images.

BROWSE FOR AN IMAGE

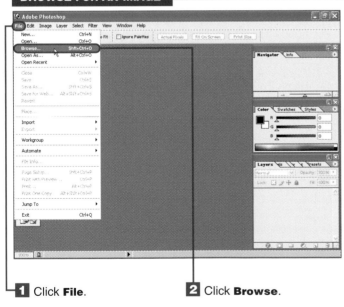

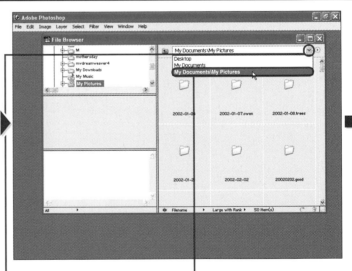

1 Click **File**.

2 Click **Browse**.

■ The File Browser opens.

3 Press **Tab** to hide the toolbox and palettes.

4 Click ☑ (🔁).

5 Click a location on your computer to browse.

■ The folders and files inside the location display.

Where should I store my images on my computer?

You may find it helpful to keep all of your images in a single folder somewhere central on your computer, such as on your desktop or inside your My Pictures folder (or your Documents or Pictures folder on a Macintosh). You may want to create subfolders named with dates or subjects to further organize the images. Keeping images in one place makes it easy to access them from Photoshop.

6 Double-click a folder to open it.

■ The contents of the folder displays.

■ Thumbnail previews display for the image files.

7 Double-click an image file to open it.

■ The image opens.

■ You can also click and drag an image file from the File Browser to the work area to open it.

■ You can press Tab to show the toolbox and palettes.

CREATE A NEW IMAGE

You can start a Photoshop project by creating a blank image.

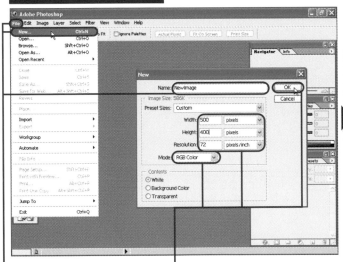

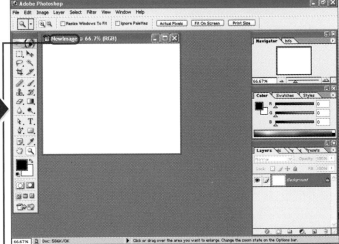

1 Click **File**.

2 Click **New**.

■ The New dialog box displays.

3 Type a name for the new image.

4 Type in the desired dimensions and resolution.

5 Click ☑ (⬧) and select a color mode.

Note: See Chapter 6 for more about color modes.

6 Click **OK**.

■ Photoshop creates a new image window at the specified dimensions.

■ The filename appears in the title bar.

7 Use Photoshop's tools and commands to create your image.

Note: To save your image, see Chapter 15.

EXIT PHOTOSHOP

You can exit Photoshop after you finish using the application.

EXIT PHOTOSHOP

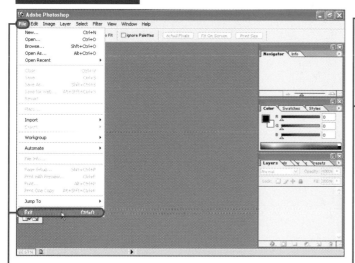

EXIT PHOTOSHOP ON A PC OR MAC OS 9

1 Click **File**.

2 Click **Exit** (**Quit**).

■ Photoshop exits.

■ Before exiting, Photoshop alerts you to any open images that have unsaved changes so you can save them.

Note: See Chapter 15 to save image files.

EXIT PHOTOSHOP IN MAC OS X

1 Click **Photoshop**.

2 Click **Quit Photoshop**.

■ Photoshop exits.

■ Before exiting, Photoshop alerts you to any open images that have unsaved changes so you can save them.

Note: See Chapter 15 to save image files.

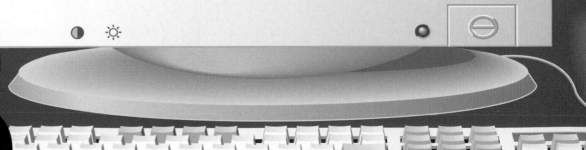

CHAPTER 2

Understanding Photoshop Basics

Are you ready to start working with images? This chapter shows you how to select tools and fine-tune your workspace.

MAGNIFY WITH THE ZOOM TOOL

You can change the magnification of an image with the Zoom tool. This allows you to view small details in an image or view an image at full size.

MAGNIFY WITH THE ZOOM TOOL

INCREASE MAGNIFICATION

1 Click the Zoom tool (⌕).

2 Click the image.

■ Photoshop increases the magnification of the image.

■ The point that you clicked in the image is centered in the window.

■ The current magnification shows in the title bar and status bar.

■ You can choose an exact magnification by typing a percentage value in the status bar.

How do I quickly return an image to 100% magnification?

Double-click  in the toolbox, click **Actual Pixels** on the Options bar, or click **View** and then **Actual Pixels** from the menu.

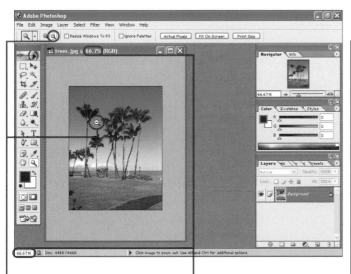

DECREASE MAGNIFICATION

1 Click the Zoom Out button ( ).

2 Click the image.

■ Photoshop decreases the magnification of the image.

■ The current magnification shows in the title bar and status bar.

■ You can also press and hold **Alt** (**option**) and click the image to decrease magnification.

MAGNIFY A DETAIL

1 Click the Zoom In button ( ).

2 Click and drag with the Zoom tool to select the detail.

■ The detail appears enlarged on-screen.

ADJUST VIEWS

You can move an image within the window by using the Hand tool or scroll bars. The Hand tool helps you navigate to an exact area on the image.

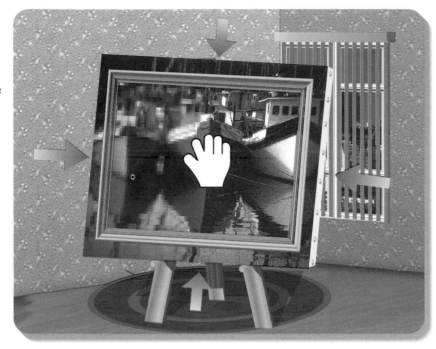

The Hand tool is a more flexible alternative to using the scroll bars because, unlike the scroll bars, the Hand tool enables you to drag the image freely in two dimensions.

ADJUST VIEWS

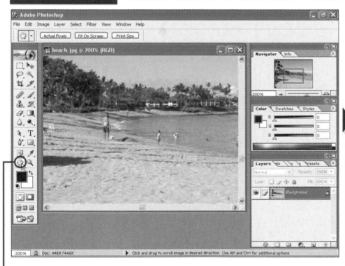

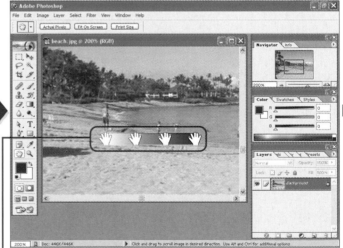

USING THE HAND TOOL

1 Click the Hand tool ([🖐]).

Note: For [🖐] to produce an effect, the image must be larger than the image window.

2 Click and drag inside the image window.

How can I quickly adjust the image window to see the entire image at its largest possible magnification on-screen?

You have three different ways to magnify the image to its largest possible size: By double-clicking , by clicking the **Fit On Screen** button on the Options bar, or by clicking **View** and then **Fit on Screen** from the menu.

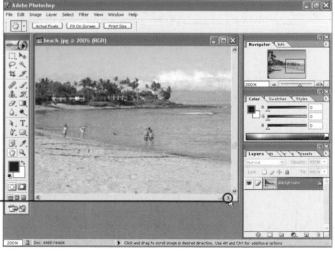

■ The view of the image shifts inside the window.

USING THE SCROLL BARS

1 Click and hold one of the window's scroll bar buttons.

■ The image scrolls.

CHANGE SCREEN MODES

You can switch the screen mode to change the look of your workspace on-screen.

CHANGE SCREEN MODES

SWITCH TO FULL SCREEN MODE

Note: The standard screen mode lets you view multiple images at once, each in a different window.

1 Click the Full Screen Mode with Menu Bar button (▣).

■ Photoshop puts the current image window in the center of a blank, full-screen canvas with the menu bar at the top of the screen.

**How do I display the menu
bar when in Full Screen
mode?**

Press `Shift` + `F` to toggle
the view of the menu bar in
Full Screen mode.

SWITCH TO FULL SCREEN

1 Click the Full Screen
Mode button (🔲).

■ The image appears full
screen without the menu bar.
The options bar, toolbox,
and palettes are still present.

CLOSE TOOLBOX AND PALETTES

1 Press `Tab`.

■ Photoshop closes all
toolboxes and palettes.

Note: The `Tab` *feature works in all
of Photoshop's screen modes.*

*Note: To view the toolbox and
palettes, you can press* `Tab` *again.*

VIEW RULERS AND GUIDES

You can turn on rulers and create guides to help accurately place elements in your image.

You can turn on a grid to place objects with even more precision. See "View a Grid" for more information.

VIEW RULERS AND GUIDES

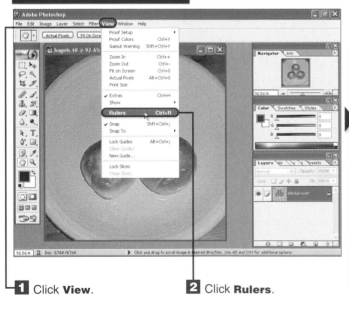

1 Click **View**.

2 Click **Rulers**.

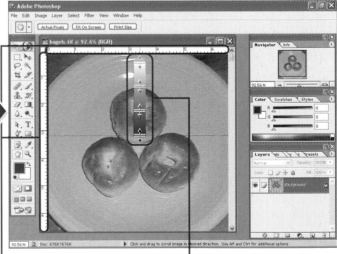

■ Photoshop adds rulers to the top and left sides of the image window.

3 Click one of the rulers and drag the cursor into the window.

How do I change the units of my rulers?

Click **Edit** (**Photoshop**, Mac OS X), **Preferences**, and then **Units & Rulers**. A dialog box appears that lets you change the units to pixels, inches, centimeters, points, picas, or percent.

■ A thin colored line called a guide appears.

Note: Guides help you position the different elements that make up your Photoshop image. These lines do not appear on the printed image.

MOVE A GUIDE

1 Click the Move tool (🕂) to adjust the placement of a guide.

2 Place the cursor over a guide and click and drag.

*Note: To align elements with the guides, click **View**, **Snap To**, and then **Guides**.*

VIEW A GRID

You can turn on a grid that overlays your image. A grid can help you precisely organize objects within your image, especially when used with rulers turned on. See the section "View Rulers and Guides," in this chapter, for more on rulers.

VIEW A GRID

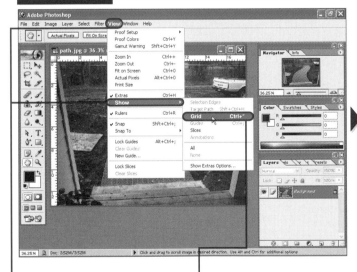

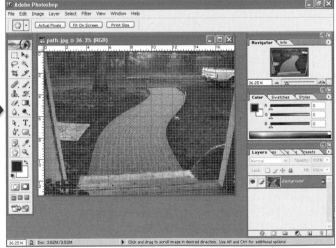

1 Click **View**.

2 Click **Show**.

3 Click **Grid**.

■ A grid appears on top of the image.

■ To adjust the space separating the grid lines, click **Edit** (**Photoshop**, Mac OS X), **Preferences**, and then **Guides**, **Grid & Slices**.

■ When you click **View**, **Snap To**, and then **Grid**, objects in an image align with the grid lines when you move the objects close to them.

You can press letter keys to select items in the toolbox. You may find this more efficient than clicking on the tools.

Each tool in the toolbox has a letter associated with it. Photoshop allows you to easily determine this letter.

USING SHORTCUTS TO SELECT TOOLS

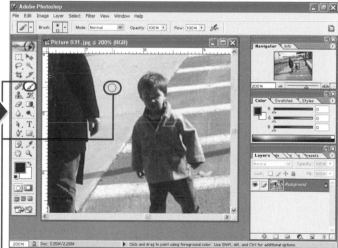

1 Place the mouse ▷ over a tool in the toolbox and hold it there.

■ A small box appears that describes the tool and gives its shortcut key.

2 Press the indicated letter to select the tool.

■ Photoshop automatically selects the tool icon in the toolbox, and ▷ becomes the new tool.

Note: You can modify the shape of the cursor by adjusting Photoshop's Preferences settings. See Chapter 1 for more information.

■ You can use the following shortcut keys for some common Photoshop tools:

Marquee	**M**	Move	**V**
Lasso	**L**	Paintbrush	**B**
Type	**T**	Zoom	**Z**

UNDO COMMANDS

You can undo multiple commands using the History palette. This allows you to correct mistakes.

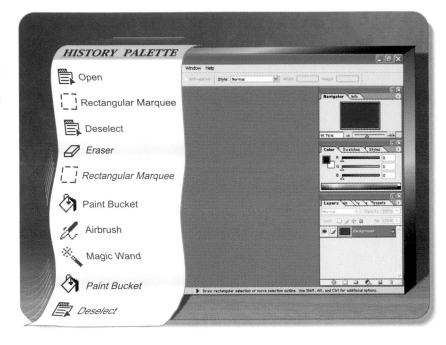

The History palette lists recently executed commands with the most recent command at the bottom.

UNDO COMMANDS

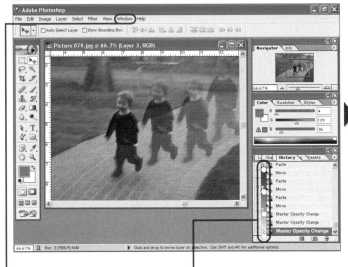 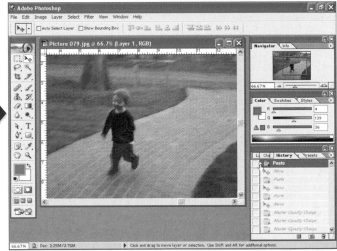

1 Click **Window**.

2 Click **History**.

3 Click and drag the History slider (▷) upward.

■ Alternatively, you can click a previous command in the history palette.

■ Photoshop undoes the previous commands.

34

REVERT AN IMAGE

You can revert an image
to the previously saved
state. This allows you to
start your image editing
over.

REVERT AN IMAGE

1 Click **File**.

2 Click **Revert**.

■ Photoshop reverts the
image to its previously
saved state.

■ You can click **Edit** and
then **Undo Revert** to return
to the unreverted state.

The Nature Preserve

Join us for a journey through the World Wide Web!

Home   Cats' Corner   Birds' Nest   Nature Paradises

CHAPTER 3

Changing the Size of an Image

Would you like to change the size of your image? This chapter shows you how to change the on-screen or print size and print resolution as well as how to crop an image.

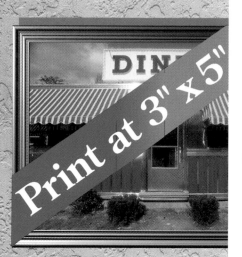

CHANGE THE ON-SCREEN SIZE OF AN IMAGE

You can change the size at which an image displays on your computer monitor so that viewers can see the entire image.

Because you lose less detail when you decrease an image's size than when you increase it, consider starting with an image that is too big rather than with one that is too small.

CHANGE THE ON-SCREEN SIZE OF AN IMAGE

1 Click **Image**.

2 Click **Image Size**.

■ The Image Size dialog box appears, listing the on-screen height and width of the image.

■ To resize by a certain percentage, click ▼ (⬍) and change the units to **percent**.

3 Make sure **Resample Image** is checked (☐ changes to ☑).

Note: Resampling is the process of increasing or decreasing the number of pixels in an image as its size changes.

What is the difference between an image's on-screen size and its print size?

On-screen size depends only on the number of pixels that make up an image. Print size depends on the number of pixels as well as the print resolution, which is the density of the pixels on a printed page. Higher resolutions print a smaller image, while lower resolutions print a larger image, given the same on-screen size.

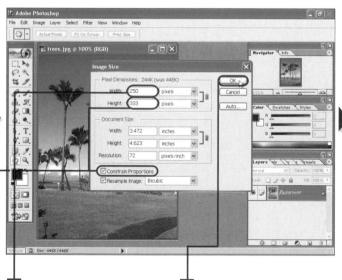

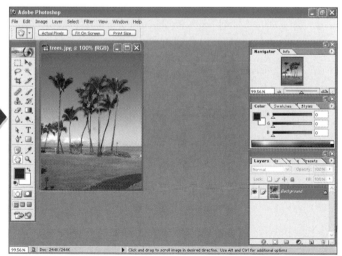

4 Type a size for a dimension.

■ Click **Constrain Proportions** (☐ changes to ☑) to allow the other dimension to change proportionally.

5 Click **OK**.

■ You can restore the original dialog box settings by holding down Alt (option) and clicking **Cancel**, which changes to **Reset**.

■ Photoshop resizes the image.

Note: Changing the number of pixels in an image can add blur. To sharpen a resized image, apply the Unsharp Mask filter as covered in Chapter 11.

CHANGE THE PRINT SIZE OF AN IMAGE

You can change the printed size of an image to determine how it appears on paper.

CHANGE THE PRINT SIZE OF AN IMAGE

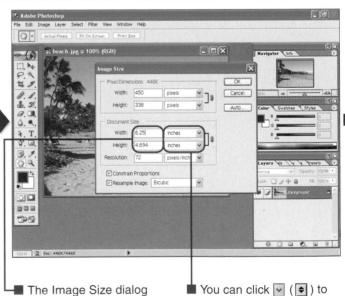

1 Click **Image**.

2 Click **Image Size**.

■ The Image Size dialog box appears, listing the current height and width of the printed image.

■ You can click ⏷ (⬍) to change the unit of measurement.

How do I preview an image's printed size?

Click **File** and then click **Print with Preview**. A dialog box displays how the image will print on the page. There are also commands that let you adjust the size and positioning of the image. Mac OS X users can also view previews of their printouts by clicking **Preview** in the Print dialog box. This creates a temporary PDF that opens in the Preview application. See Chapter 16 for more information on printing images.

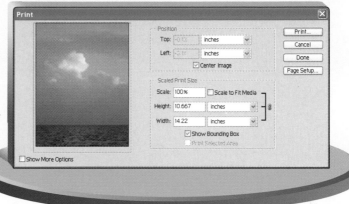

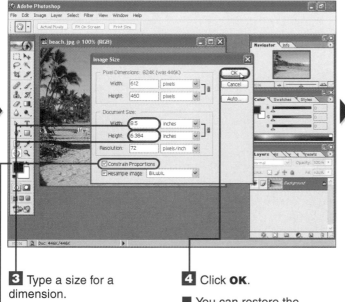

3 Type a size for a dimension.

■ You can click **Constrain Proportions** (☐ changes to ☑) to cause the other dimension to change proportionally.

4 Click **OK**.

■ You can restore the original dialog box settings by holding down Alt (option) and clicking **Cancel**, which changes to **Reset**.

■ Photoshop resizes the image.

Note: Changing the number of pixels in an image can add blur. To sharpen a resized image, apply the Unsharp Mask filter as covered in Chapter 11.

41

CHANGE THE RESOLUTION OF AN IMAGE

You can change the print resolution of an image to increase or decrease the print quality.

72 dpi

300 dpi

The resolution, combined with the number of pixels in an image, determines the size of a printed image.

The greater the resolution, the better the image looks on the printed page — up to a limit, which varies with the type of printer.

CHANGE THE RESOLUTION OF AN IMAGE

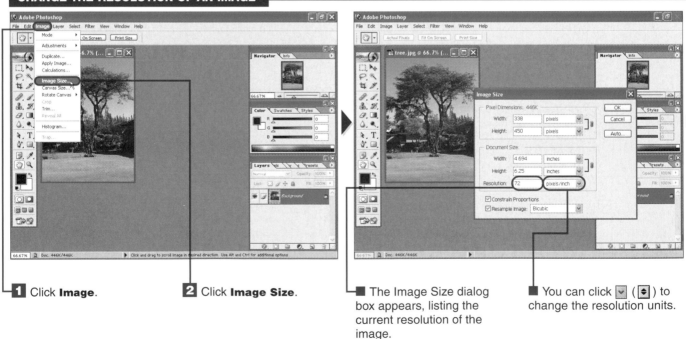

1 Click **Image**.

2 Click **Image Size**.

■ The Image Size dialog box appears, listing the current resolution of the image.

■ You can click ⮟ (⬍) to change the resolution units.

What is the relationship between resolution, on-screen size, and print size?

To determine the printed size of a Photoshop image, you can divide the on-screen size by the resolution. If you have an image with an on-screen width of 480 pixels and a resolution of 120 pixels per inch, the printed width is 4 inches.

480 pixels / 120 pixels per inch = 4 inches

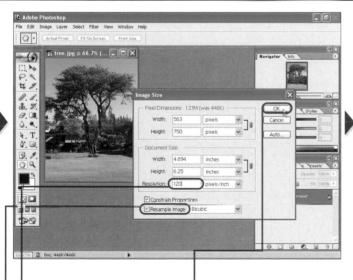

3 Type a new resolution.

■ You can click **Resample Image** (☐ changes to ☑) to adjust the number of pixels in your image and keep the print dimensions fixed.

4 Click **OK**.

■ You can restore the original dialog box settings by holding down Alt (option) and clicking **Cancel**, which changes to **Reset**.

■ In this example, because the change in resolution changes the number of pixels in the image, the on-screen image changes in size while the print size stays the same.

AUTOMATICALLY CHOOSE A RESOLUTION

You can automatically
select a resolution based
on quality requirements
and the screen size, or
resolution, of your
printer.

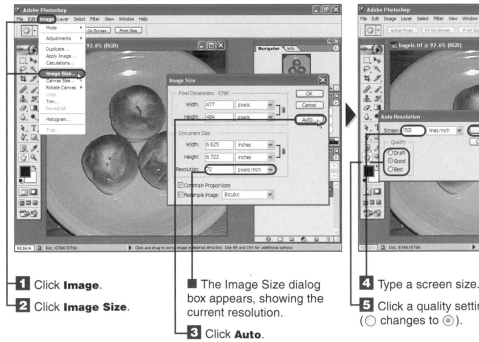

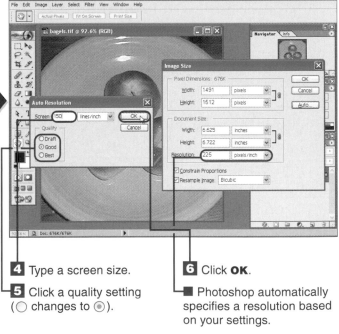

1 Click **Image**.

2 Click **Image Size**.

■ The Image Size dialog
box appears, showing the
current resolution.

3 Click **Auto**.

■ The Auto Resolution
dialog box appears.

4 Type a screen size.

5 Click a quality setting
(○ changes to ◉).

6 Click **OK**.

■ Photoshop automatically
specifies a resolution based
on your settings.

FIT AN IMAGE

You can use the Fit Image command to automatically resize an image to a specific on-screen height and width. This can be useful when you need the image to fit inside exact on-screen dimensions.

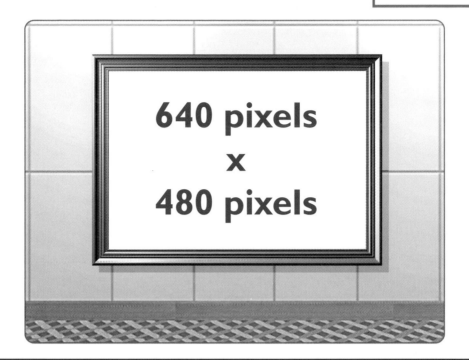

640 pixels

x

480 pixels

FIT AN IMAGE

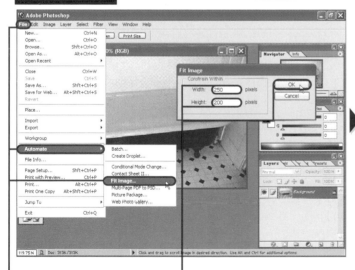

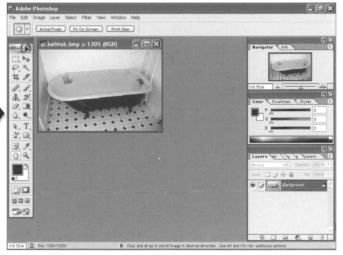

1 Click **File**.

2 Click **Automate**.

3 Click **Fit Image**.

■ The Fit Image dialog box appears.

4 Type a width.

5 Type a height.

6 Click **OK**.

■ Photoshop fits the image inside the specified dimensions, without changing the proportions of the image.

CROP AN IMAGE

You can use the Crop tool to change the size of an image to remove unneeded space on the top, bottom, and sides.

1 Click the Crop tool (![crop icon]).

2 Click and drag to select the area of the image you want to keep.

■ You can also crop an image by changing its canvas size.

Note: See the section "Change the Canvas Size of an Image" for more information.

3 Click and drag the side and corner handles (![handle]) to adjust the size of the cropping boundary.

■ You can click and drag inside the cropping boundary to move it without adjusting its size.

4 Click ![check] or press **Enter** (**Return**).

■ To exit the cropping process, you can press **Esc** (⌘ + .) or click ![cancel].

How do I increase the area of an image using the Crop tool?

Enlarge the image window to add extra space around the image. Then apply the Crop tool so that the cropping boundary extends beyond the borders of the image. When you apply cropping, the image canvas enlarges.

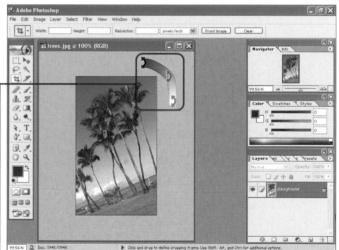

■ Photoshop crops the image, deleting the pixels outside of the cropping boundary.

ROTATE THE CROPPING AREA

1 Perform steps **1** through **3** on the previous page.

2 Click and drag outside of the boundary lines.

3 Click ✓ or press **Enter** (**Return**).

■ Photoshop rotates the cropping boundary.

CHANGE THE CANVAS SIZE OF AN IMAGE

You can alter the canvas size of an image in order to change its rectangular shape or add blank space around its borders.

The *canvas* is the area on which an image sits. Changing the canvas size is one way to crop an image.

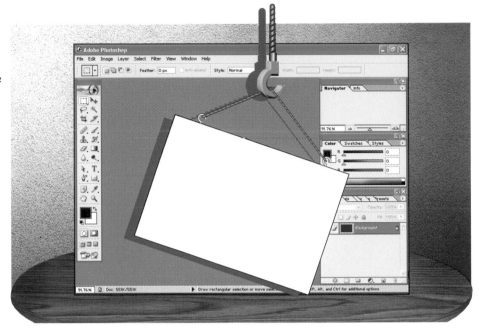

The Crop tool gives you an alternative to changing the canvas size. See the section "Crop an Image" for more information.

CHANGE THE CANVAS SIZE OF AN IMAGE

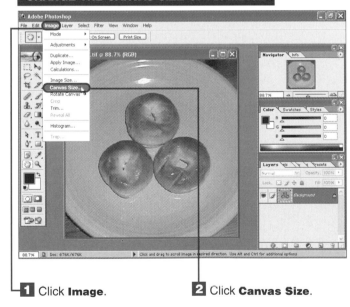

1 Click **Image**.

2 Click **Canvas Size**.

■ The Canvas Size dialog box appears, listing the current dimensions of the canvas.

■ You can click ⊡ (⊡) to change the unit of measurement.

Why would I want to change the canvas size instead of using the Crop tool?

Changing the canvas size can be useful when you want to change the size of an image precisely. You can specify the exact number of pixels that Photoshop adds or subtracts around the border. With the Crop tool, it can be more difficult to make changes with pixel precision.

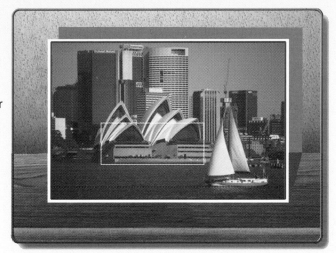

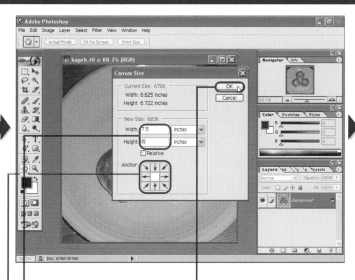

3 Type the new canvas dimensions.

■ You can modify in which directions Photoshop changes the canvas size by selecting an anchor point.

4 Click **OK**.

*Note: If you decrease a dimension, Photoshop displays a dialog box asking whether you want to proceed. Click **Proceed**.*

■ Photoshop changes the image's canvas size.

■ Because the middle anchor point is selected in this example, the canvas size changes equally on opposite sides.

■ Photoshop fills any new canvas space with the background color — in this case, white.

CHAPTER 4

Making Selections

Do you want to move, color, or transform parts of your image independently from the rest of the image? The first step is to make a selection. This chapter shows you how.

SELECT WITH THE MARQUEE TOOLS

You can select a rectangular or elliptical area of your image by using the Marquee tools. Then you can move, delete, or stylize the selected area using other Photoshop commands.

SELECT WITH THE MARQUEE TOOLS

USING THE RECTANGULAR MARQUEE TOOL

1 Click the Rectangular Marquee tool ([ ]).

2 Click and drag diagonally inside the image window.

■ You can hold down **Shift** while you click and drag to create a square selection.

■ Photoshop selects a rectangular portion of your image. You can now perform other commands on the selection.

■ You can deselect a selection by clicking **Select** and then **Deselect**.

How do I customize the Marquee tools?

You can customize the Marquee tools ([□] and [○]) by using the boxes and menus in the Options bar. Typing in a Feather value softens your selection edge — which means that Photoshop partially selects pixels near the edge. The Style list lets you define your Marquee tool as a fixed size. You define the fixed dimensions in the Width and Height boxes.

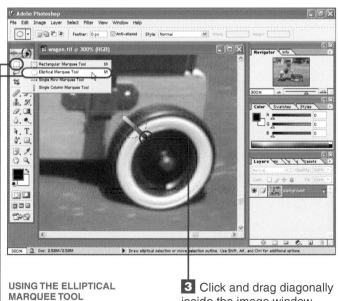

USING THE ELLIPTICAL MARQUEE TOOL

1 Click and hold [□].

2 From the box that appears, click the Elliptical Marquee tool ([○]).

3 Click and drag diagonally inside the image window.

■ You can hold down **Shift** while you click and drag to create a circular selection.

■ Photoshop selects an elliptical portion of your image. You can now perform other commands on the selection.

■ You can deselect a selection by clicking **Select** and then **Deselect**.

SELECT WITH THE LASSO TOOL

You can create oddly shaped selections with the Lasso tools. Then you can move, delete, or stylize the selected area using other Photoshop commands.

You can use the regular Lasso tool to create curved selections. The Polygonal Lasso tool lets you easily create a selection made up of many straight lines.

SELECT WITH THE LASSO TOOL

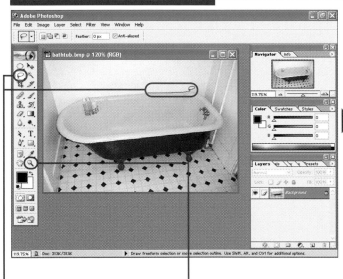

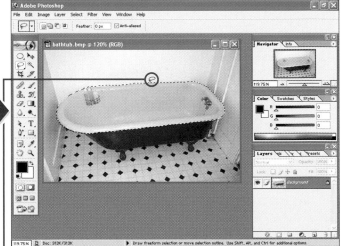

USING THE REGULAR LASSO

1 Click the Lasso tool (⌾).

2 Click and drag with your cursor (⌾) to make a selection.

■ To accurately trace a complicated edge, you can magnify that part of the image with the Zoom tool (🔍).

Note: See Chapter 2 for more on the Zoom tool.

3 Drag to the beginning point and release the mouse button.

■ The selection is now complete.

What if my lasso selection is not as precise as I want it to be?

You may find selecting complicated outlines with the Lasso tool (⬚) difficult, even for the steadiest of hands. To fix an imprecise Lasso selection, you can

■ Deselect the selection, by clicking **Select** and then **Deselect**, and try again.

■ Try to fix your selection. See "Add to or Subtract from Your Selection."

■ Switch to the magnetic lasso. See "Select with the Magnetic Lasso Tool."

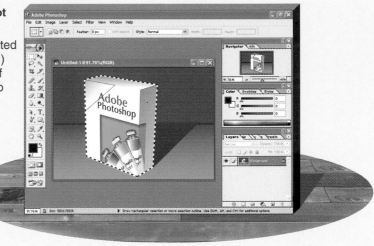

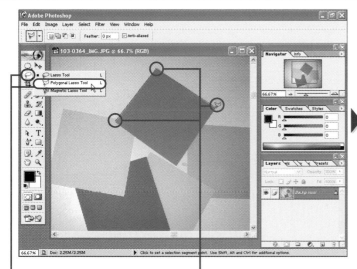

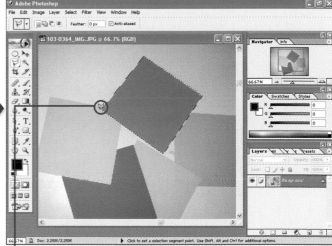

USING THE POLYGONAL LASSO

1 Click and hold ⬚.

2 Click the Polygonal Lasso tool (⬚) in the box that appears.

3 Click multiple times along the border of the area you would like to select.

4 To complete the selection, click the starting point.

■ You can also double-click anywhere in the image and Photoshop adds a final straight line connected to the starting point.

■ The selection is now complete.

■ You can achieve a polygonal effect with the regular Lasso tool by pressing **Alt** (**option**) and clicking to make your selection.

SELECT WITH THE MAGNETIC LASSO TOOL

You can select elements of your image that have well-defined edges quickly and easily with the Magnetic Lasso tool.

The Magnetic Lasso works best when the element you are trying to select contrasts sharply with its background.

SELECT WITH THE MAGNETIC LASSO TOOL

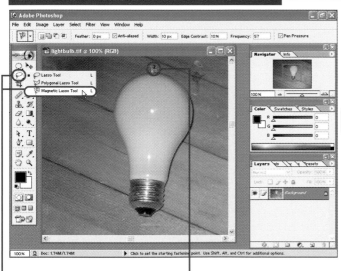

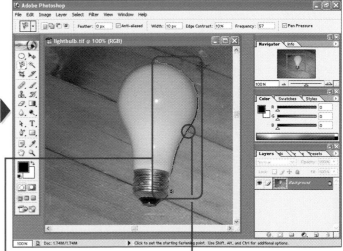

1 Click and hold 🔲.

2 Click the Magnetic Lasso tool (🔲) from the box that appears.

3 Click the edge of the object you want to select.

■ This creates a beginning anchor point.

4 Drag your cursor (🔲) along the edge of the object.

■ The Magnetic Lasso's path snaps to the edge of the element as you drag.

■ To help guide the lasso, you can click to add anchor points as you go along the path.

How can I adjust the precision of the Magnetic Lasso tool?

You can use the Options bar to adjust the Magnetic Lasso tool's precision:

■ **Width:** The number of nearby pixels the lasso considers when creating a selection.

■ **Edge Contrast:** How much contrast is required for the lasso to consider something an edge.

■ **Frequency:** The frequency of the anchor points.

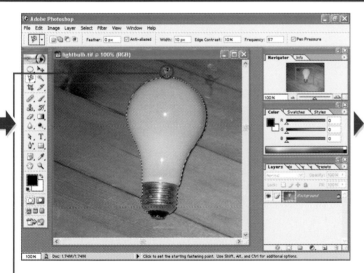

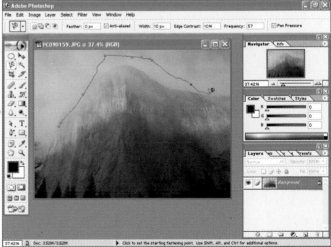

5 Click the beginning anchor point to finish your selection.

■ Alternatively, you can double-click anywhere in the image and Photoshop completes the selection for you.

■ The path is complete.

■ This example shows that the Magnetic Lasso is less useful for selecting areas where you find little contrast between the image and its background.

SELECT WITH THE MAGIC WAND TOOL

You can select groups of similarly colored pixels with the Magic Wand tool. You may find this useful if you wish to remove an object from a background.

You can control how particular the tool is by selecting a tolerance value from 0 to 255.

SELECT WITH THE MAGIC WAND TOOL

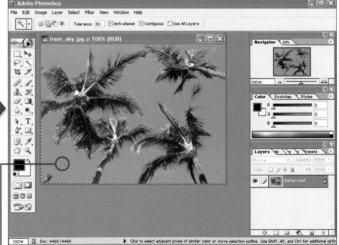

1 Click the Magic Wand tool ([✦]).

2 Type a number from 0 to 255 into the Tolerance field.

■ To select a narrow range of colors, type a small number; to select a wide range of colors, type a large number.

3 Click the area you want to select inside the image.

■ Photoshop selects the pixel you clicked, plus any similarly colored pixels near it.

**With what type of images does
the Magic Wand work best?**

The Magic Wand tool (✳) works
best with images that have areas
of solid color. The Magic Wand
tool is less helpful with images
that contain subtle shifts in color
or color gradients.

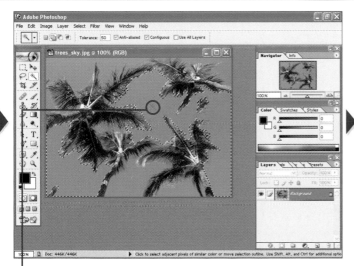

4 To add to your selection,
press **Shift** and click
elsewhere in the image.

■ Photoshop adds to your
selection.

5 To delete the selected
pixels, press **Delete**.

■ Photoshop replaces the
pixels with the background
color.

■ In this example, Photoshop
replaces the pixels with white.

■ If you make the selection in
a layer, the deleted selection
becomes transparent. See
Chapter 9 for more about
layers.

SELECT WITH THE COLOR RANGE COMMAND

You can select a set range of colors within an image with the Color Range command. This allows you to quickly select a region of relatively solid color, such as a sky or a blank wall.

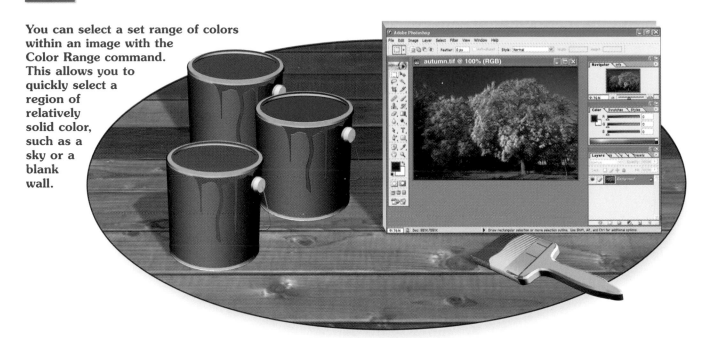

SELECT WITH THE COLOR RANGE COMMAND

1 Click **Select**.

2 Click **Color Range**.

■ The Color Range dialog box appears.

3 Click inside the image window.

■ Photoshop selects all the pixels in the image that are similar to the pixel you clicked. These areas turn white in the Color Range window.

■ The number of pixels that turn white depends on the Fuzziness setting.

How do I limit the area of the image affected by the Color Range?

Select an area of the image — by using the Marquee, Lasso, or other tool — before clicking **Select** and then **Color Range**.

4 To increase the range of color, click and drag the Fuzziness slider (△) to the right.

■ You can decrease the color range by dragging the slider to the left.

■ You can also broaden the selected area by clicking the Add eyedropper (🖉) and then clicking other parts of the image.

5 Click **OK** to make a selection in the main image window.

■ Photoshop makes the selection.

■ Sometimes the color range command selects unwanted areas of the image. To eliminate these areas, see "Add to or Subtract from Your Selection."

SELECT ALL THE PIXELS IN AN IMAGE

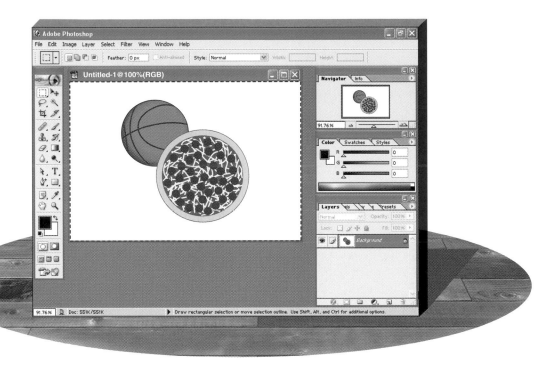

You can select all the pixels in an image by using a single command. This lets you perform a command on the entire image, such as copying it to a different image window.

With the entire image window selected, you can easily delete your image.

SELECT ALL THE PIXELS IN AN IMAGE

1 Click **Select**.

2 Click **All**.

■ You can also press Ctrl + A (⌘ + A) to select all the pixels in an image.

■ Photoshop selects the entire image window.

■ You can delete your image by pressing Delete.

■ To copy your image, press Ctrl + C (⌘ + C).

■ To paste your image, press Ctrl + V (⌘ + V).

MOVE A SELECTION BORDER

You can move a selection border if your original selection is not in the intended place.

MOVE A SELECTION BORDER

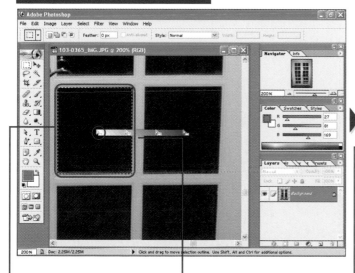

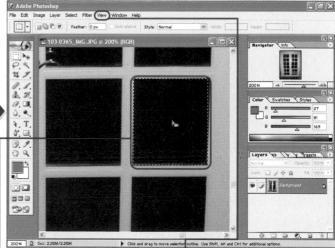

1 Make a selection with a selection tool (⬚, ◯, or ✦).

Note: To learn more about the various selection tools, see the previous sections in this chapter.

2 Click and drag inside the selection.

■ The selection border moves.

■ You can hide a selection by clicking **View** and then **Selection Edges**.

ADD TO OR SUBTRACT FROM YOUR SELECTION

You can add to or
subtract from your
selection by using
various selection tools.

ADD TO A SELECTION

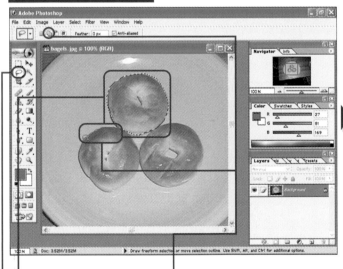

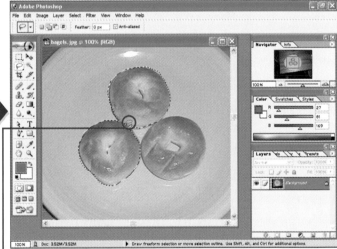

1 Make a selection using
one of Photoshop's selection
tools.

■ The selection in this
example illustrates the use
of the Lasso tool (⬚).

2 Click a selection tool.

*Note: See the previous sections in
this chapter to select the appropriate
tool for your image.*

3 Click the Add to
Selection button (⬚).

4 Select the area you want
to add.

5 Complete the selection
by closing the path.

■ The original selection
enlarges.

■ You can enlarge the
selection further by repeating
steps **2** through **5**.

■ You can also add to a
selection by pressing **Shift**
as you make your selection.

What tools can I use to add to or subtract from a selection?

You can use any of the Marquee, Lasso, or Magic Wand tools, discussed in previous sections in this chapter, to add to or subtract from a selection. All three have Add to Selection and Subtract from Selection buttons available in the Options bar when you select them.

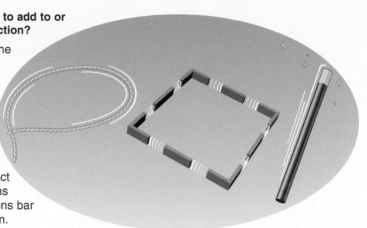

SUBTRACT FROM A SELECTION

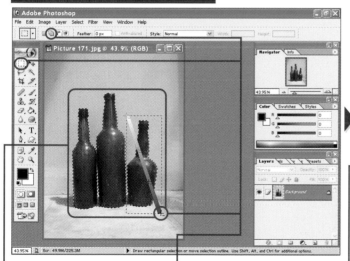

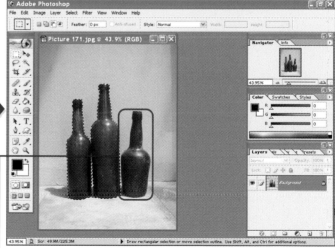

1 Make a selection using one of Photoshop's selection tools.

■ The selection in this example illustrates the use of the Rectangular Marquee tool ([ ]).

2 Click a selection tool.

3 Click the Subtract from Selection button ([ ]).

4 Select the area you want to subtract.

■ Photoshop deselects, or subtracts, the selected area.

■ You can subtract other parts of the selection by repeating steps **2** through **4**.

■ You can also subtract from a selection by holding down **Alt** (**option**) as you make your selection.

EXPAND OR CONTRACT SELECTIONS

You can expand or contract a selection by a set number of pixels. This lets you easily fine-tune your selections.

You can expand or contract a selection up to 100 pixels at a time.

EXPAND A SELECTION

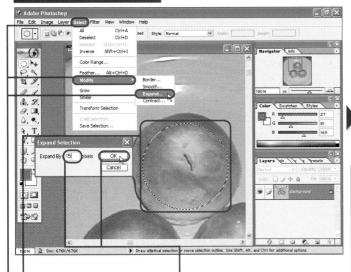

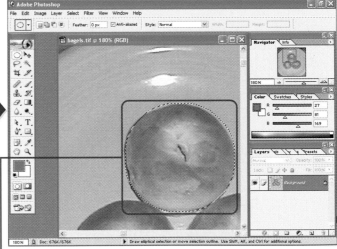

1 Make a selection using one of Photoshop's selection tools.

2 Click **Select**.

3 Click **Modify**.

4 Click **Expand**.

■ The Expand Selection dialog box appears.

5 Type a value in the Expand By field.

6 Click **OK**.

■ Photoshop expands the selection by the specified number of pixels.

■ You can repeat steps **2** through **6** to expand a selection further.

How can I smooth the edges of a selection?

Make your selection and then click **Select**, **Modify**, and **Smooth**. Type a Sample Radius value. The greater the value, the more Photoshop smoothes the selection.

CONTRACT A SELECTION

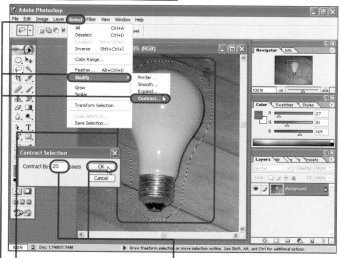

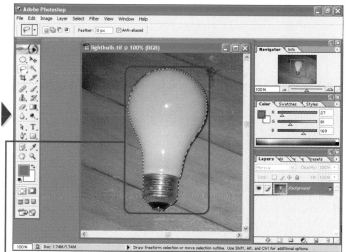

1 Make a selection using one of Photoshop's selection tools.

2 Click **Select**.

3 Click **Modify**.

4 Click **Contract**.

■ The Contract Selection dialog box appears.

5 Type a value in the Contract By field.

6 Click **OK**.

■ Photoshop contracts the selection by the number of pixels specified.

■ You can repeat steps **2** through **6** to contract a selection further.

INVERT A SELECTION

You can invert a selection to deselect what is currently selected and select everything else. This is useful when you want to select a background around an object.

1 Make a selection using one of Photoshop's selection tools.

Note: To learn more about the various selection tools, see the previous sections in this chapter.

2 Click **Select**.

3 Click **Inverse**.

■ Photoshop inverts the selection.

GROW A SELECTION

You can increase the size
of your selection using
the Grow command,
which is useful when you
want to include similarly
colored, neighboring
pixels in your selection.

GROW A SELECTION

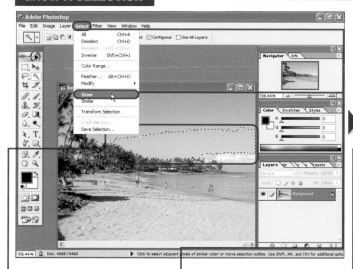

1 Make a selection using
one of Photoshop's selection
tools.

*Note: To learn more about the
various selection tools, see the
previous sections in this chapter.*

2 Click **Select**.

3 Click **Grow**.

■ The selection grows to
include similarly colored
pixels contiguous with the
current selection.

■ To include noncontiguous
pixels as well, you can click
Select and then **Similar**.

■ You can change the
number of similarly colored
pixels the Grow command
selects by changing the
Tolerance setting. Click the
Magic Wand tool, type a new
value in the Tolerance field,
make your selection, click
Select and then **Grow**.

CREATE SLICES

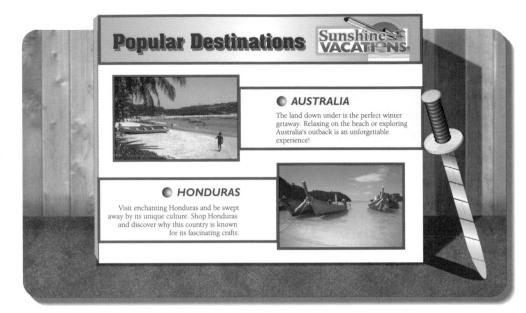

You can divide a large image that you want to display on the Web into smaller rectangular sections called *slices*. The different slices of an image can then be optimized independently of one another for faster download. See Chapter 15 for details.

Slices can also be used to create special Web effects, such as animations and rollovers, in ImageReady. ImageReady is a Web imaging program that comes with Photoshop.

CREATE SLICES

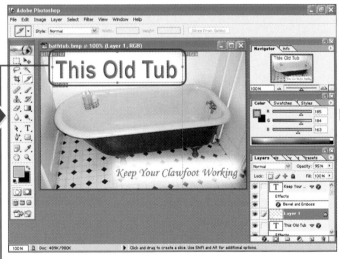

1 Click the Slice tool ( ).

2 Click and drag inside the image to create a slice.

■ Photoshop creates a slice where you clicked and dragged.

Note: Slices you define are called user-slices.

■ Photoshop fills in the rest of the image with auto-slices.

Note: User-slices remain fixed when you add more slices to your image, whereas auto-slices can change size.

How do I resize or delete slices in my image?

First, select the Slice Select tool (✎), which is accessible by clicking and holding ✎ . To resize a user-slice, click inside it and then click and drag a border handle. To delete a user-slice, click inside it and then press Delete .

3 Click and drag to define another slice in your image.

■ Photoshop creates another slice where you clicked and dragged.

■ Photoshop creates or rearranges auto-slices to fill in the rest of the image.

■ To save the different slices for the Web, see Chapter 15.

■ To learn about how to use slices in ImageReady, see Photoshop's Help information. See Chapter 1 to access Photoshop Help.

APPLYING DISTORT

PASTING SELECTION IN NEW WINDOW

DELETING SELECTION

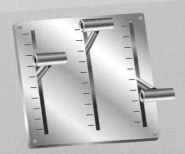

IMAGE   CLOSE

...NOW APPLYING TRANSFORMATION...

MOVE
SELECTION

CHAPTER 5

Manipulating Selections

Making a selection defines a specific area of your Photoshop image. This chapter shows you how to move, stretch, erase, and manipulate your selection in a variety of ways.

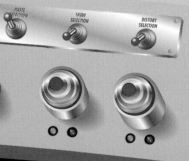

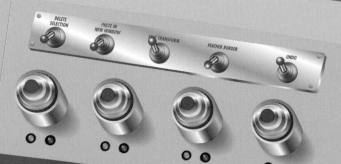

MOVE A SELECTION

You can move a selection by using the Move tool, which lets you rearrange elements of your image.

You can move elements of your image that are in the background layer or in other layers. For details about layers, see Chapter 9.

MOVE A SELECTION

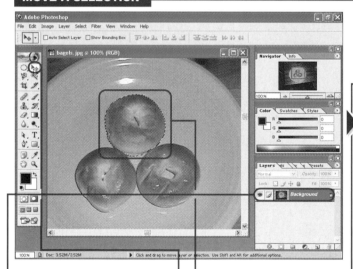

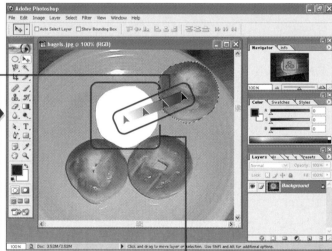

MOVE A SELECTION IN THE BACKGROUND

1 Click the background layer in the Layers palette.

■ If you start with a newly scanned image, Photoshop makes the background layer the only layer.

2 Make a selection with a selection tool.

Note: See Chapter 4 for more on using selection tools, and Chapter 9 for more on layers.

3 Click the Move tool ( ).

4 Click inside the selection and drag.

■ Photoshop fills the original location of the selection with the current background color.

■ In this example, white is the default background color.

How do I move a selection in a straight line?

Hold down the **Shift** key while you drag with the Move tool (). Doing so constrains the movement of your selection horizontally, vertically, or diagonally — depending on the direction you drag.

MOVE A SELECTION IN A LAYER

1 Click a layer in the Layers palette.

2 Make a selection with a selection tool.

Note: See Chapter 4 for more on using selection tools, and Chapter 9 for more on layers.

3 Click .

4 Click inside the selection and drag.

■ Photoshop moves the selection in the layer.

■ Photoshop fills the original location of the selection with transparent pixels.

Note: Unlike the background — Photoshop's opaque default layer — layers can include transparent pixels.

COPY AND PASTE A SELECTION

You can copy a selection and make a duplicate of it somewhere else in the image.

COPY AND PASTE A SELECTION

USING THE KEYBOARD AND MOUSE

1 Make a selection with a selection tool.

Note: See Chapter 4 for more on using selection tools.

2 Click [+].

3 Press **Alt** (**option**) while you click and drag the selection.

4 Release the mouse button to "drop" the selection.

■ Photoshop creates a duplicate of the selection, which appears in the new location.

How can I copy a selection from one window to another?

Click 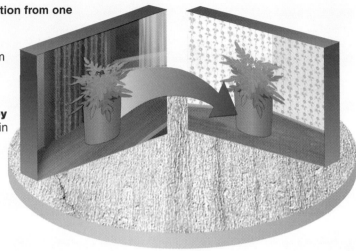 and click and drag your selection from one window to another. You can also copy selections between windows using the **Copy** and **Paste** commands in the **Edit** menu.

USING THE COPY AND PASTE COMMANDS

1 Make a selection with a selection tool.

Note: See Chapter 4 for more on using selection tools.

2 Click **Edit**.

3 Click **Copy**.

4 Using a selection tool, select where you want to paste the copied element.

■ If you do not select an area, Photoshop pastes the copy over the original.

5 Click **Edit**.

6 Click **Paste**.

■ Photoshop pastes the copy into a new layer, which you can now move independently of the original image.

Note: See "Move a Selection" for more on moving your image.

DELETE A SELECTION

You can delete a selection to remove elements from your image.

DELETE A SELECTION

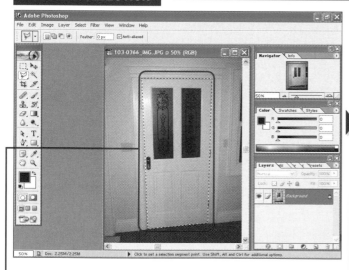

1 Make a selection with a selection tool.

Note: See Chapter 4 for more on using selection tools.

2 Press .

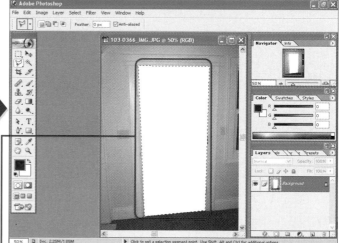

■ Photoshop deletes the selection.

■ If you are working in the background layer, the empty selection fills with the background color — in this example, white, the default background color.

■ If you are working in a nonbackground layer, deleting a selection turns the selected pixels transparent.

Note: See Chapter 9 for more about layers.

You can rotate a
selection to tilt or turn
an element upside down
in your image.

ROTATE A SELECTION

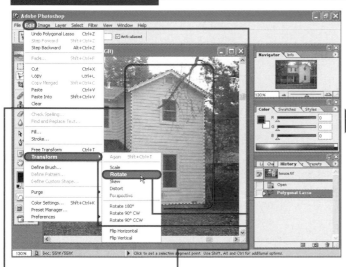

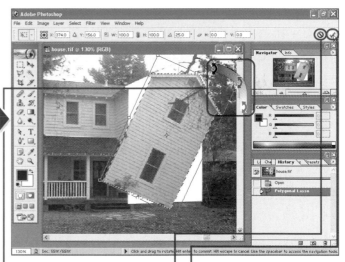

1 Make a selection with a
selection tool.

*Note: See Chapter 4 for more on
using selection tools.*

2 Click **Edit**.

3 Click **Transform**.

4 Click **Rotate**.

■ A *bounding box*, a
rectangular box with handles
on the sides and corners,
surrounds the selection.

5 Click and drag to the side
of the selection.

■ The selection rotates.

6 Click ✓ or press `Enter`
(`Return`) to commit the
rotation.

■ You can click ⊘ or press
`Esc` (⌘+.) to cancel.

SCALE A SELECTION

You can scale a selection to make it larger or smaller. Scaling allows you to emphasize parts of your image.

SCALE A SELECTION

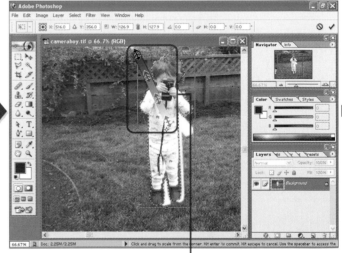

1 Make a selection with a selection tool.

Note: See Chapter 4 for more on using selection tools.

2 Click **Edit**.

3 Click **Transform**.

4 Click **Scale**.

■ A rectangular bounding box with handles on the sides and corners surrounds the selection.

5 Click and drag a corner handle to scale both the horizontal and vertical axes.

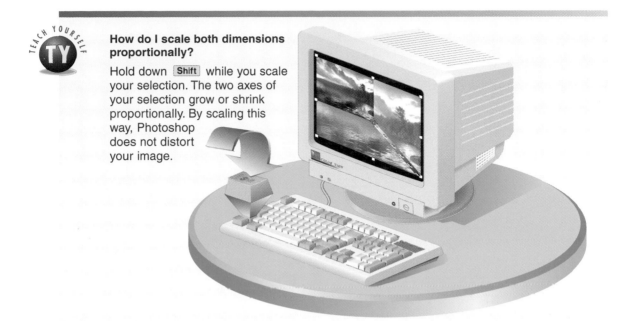

How do I scale both dimensions proportionally?

Hold down [Shift] while you scale your selection. The two axes of your selection grow or shrink proportionally. By scaling this way, Photoshop does not distort your image.

6 Click and drag a side handle to scale one axis at a time.

■ To cancel, you can click ⊘ or press [Esc] (⌘ + [.]).

■ Photoshop scales the selection to the new dimensions.

7 To apply the scaling, click ✓ or press [Enter] ([Return]).

SKEW OR DISTORT A SELECTION

You can transform a selection using the Skew or Distort command. This lets you stretch elements in your image into interesting shapes.

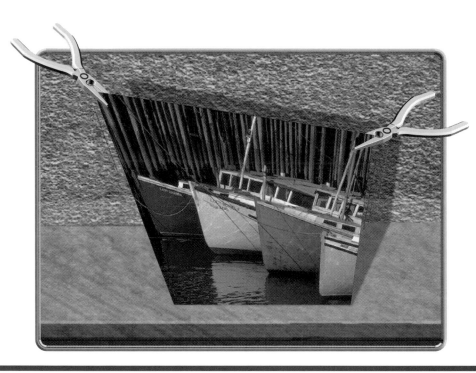

SKEW A SELECTION

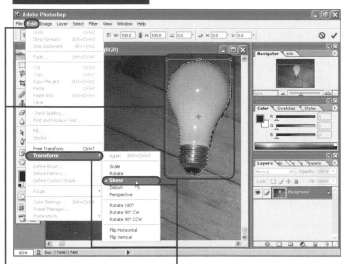

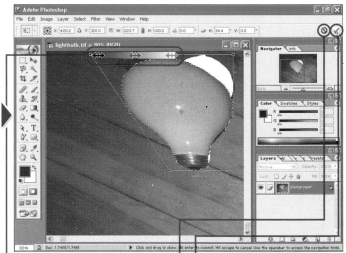

1 Make a selection with a selection tool.

Note: See Chapter 4 for more on using selection tools.

2 Click **Edit**.

3 Click **Transform**.

4 Click **Skew**.

■ A rectangular bounding box with handles on the sides and corners surrounds the selection.

5 Click and drag a handle to skew the selection.

■ Because the Skew command works along a single axis, you can drag either horizontally or vertically.

6 To apply the skewing, click ✓ or press **Enter** (**Return**).

■ To cancel, you can click ⊘ or press **Esc** (⌘+.).

How can I undo my skewing or distortion?

You can click **Edit** and then **Undo** to undo the last handle adjustment you made. This is an alternative to clicking , which cancels the entire Skew or Distort command.

DISTORT A SELECTION

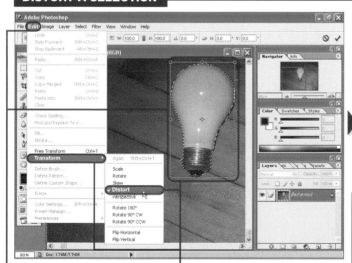

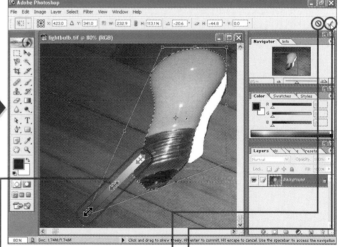

1 Make a selection with a selection tool.

Note: See Chapter 4 for more on using selection tools.

2 Click **Edit**.

3 Click **Transform**.

4 Click **Distort**.

■ A rectangular bounding box with handles on the sides and corners surrounds the selection.

5 Click and drag a handle to distort the selection.

■ The Distort command works independently of the selection's different axes; you can drag a handle both vertically and horizontally.

6 To apply the distortion, click ✔ or press **Enter** (**Return**).

■ To cancel, you can click ⊘ or press **Esc** (⌘+.).

FEATHER THE BORDER OF A SELECTION

You can feather a selection's border to create soft edges.

To soften edges, you must first select an object, feather the selection border, then delete the part of the image that surrounds your selection.

FEATHER THE BORDER OF A SELECTION

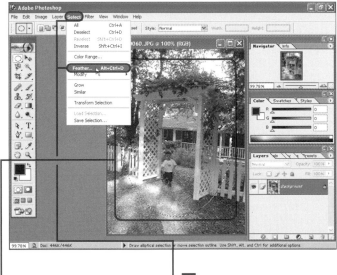

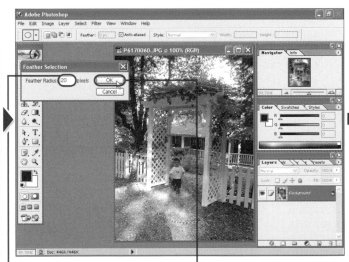

SELECT AND FEATHER AN IMAGE

1 Make a selection with a selection tool.

Note: See Chapter 4 for more on using selection tools.

2 Click **Select**.

3 Click **Feather**.

■ The Feather Selection dialog box appears.

4 Type a pixel value between 2.0 and 250 to determine the softness of the edge. The larger the number, the softer the edge.

5 Click **OK**.

What happens if I feather a selection and then apply a command to it?

Photoshop applies the command only partially to pixels near the edge of the selection.

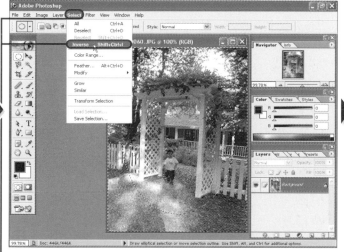

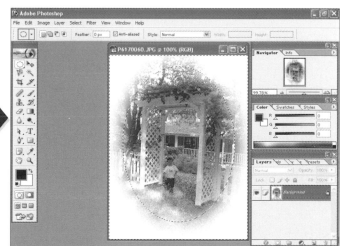

DELETE THE SURROUNDING BACKGROUND

6 Click **Select**.

7 Click **Inverse**.

■ The selection inverts, but remains feathered.

8 Press Delete.

■ You can now see the effect of the feathering.

EXTRACT AN OBJECT

You can remove objects in an image from their backgrounds using the Extract command.

1 Click **Filter**.

2 Click **Extract**.

■ Photoshop displays the image in the Extract dialog box.

■ If you make a selection before you perform the Extract command, only the selection will be displayed.

3 Click the Edge Highlighter tool ( ).

4 Highlight the edge of the object that you want to extract from the background.

■ The highlighting should overlay both the object and the background evenly.

■ You can change the size of the highlighter. For defined edges, use a smaller brush size; for fuzzier edges, use a larger brush size.

My extraction has rough edges. What can I do?

You can improve a less-than-perfect extraction by clicking **Show** and then **Original** in the Extract dialog box. Click **Show Highlight** and **Show Fill** (☐ changes to ☑). You can then edit your work. Click ✐ to erase any errant highlighting, and then rehighlight those edges with the highlighter (✐). Adjusting the value from 0 to 100 in the Smooth box can also help fine-tune the extraction process.

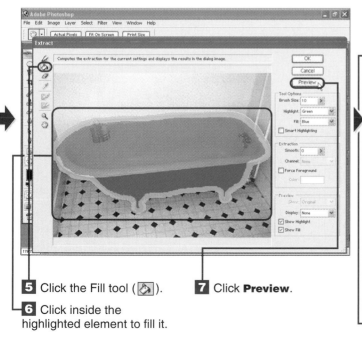

5 Click the Fill tool (🪣).

6 Click inside the highlighted element to fill it.

7 Click **Preview**.

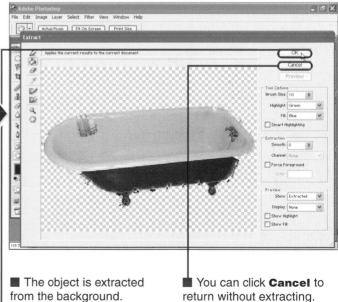

■ The object is extracted from the background.

8 Click **OK** to return to the original image window with the element extracted.

■ You can click **Cancel** to return without extracting.

CHAPTER 6

Specifying Color Modes

Would you like to reduce the number of colors in your image or convert a color image to black and white? This chapter shows you how by specifying different color modes for your images.

GREEN

RED

BLUE

WORK IN RGB MODE

You can work with a color image in RGB mode. RGB is the most common mode for working with color images in Photoshop.

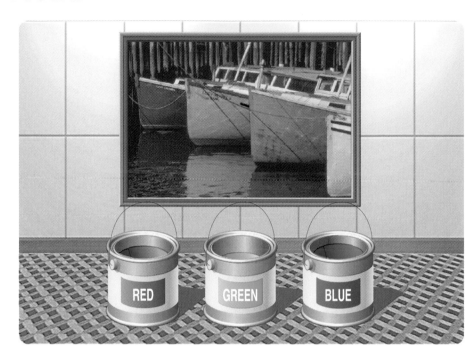

RGB stands for Red, Green, Blue. In RGB mode, the image is stored as a combination of these three primary colors.

WORK IN RGB MODE

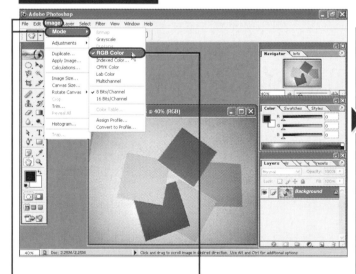

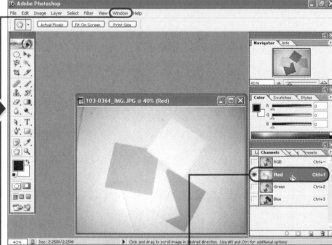

1 Click **Image**.

2 Click **Mode**.

3 Click **RGB Color**.

■ *RGB* is displayed in the image's title bar.

■ You can view the different color components of an RGB image with the Channels palette.

4 Click **Window**.

5 Click **Channels**.

■ The Channels palette displays.

6 Click the Red channel.

■ A grayscale version of the image displays the amount of red the image contains. Lighter areas mean lots of red; darker areas mean very little red.

What is CMYK mode?

Photoshop's CMYK mode represents an image's color information as a mix of **cyan** (C), **magenta** (M), **yellow** (Y), and **black** (K). You can use CMYK mode when your image needs to undergo color separation in preparation for commercial offset printing. To switch to CMYK mode, click **Image**, **Mode**, and then **CMYK Color**. Many inkjet printers are CMYK as well.

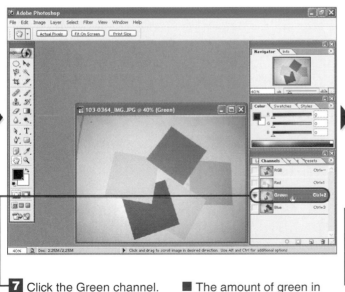

7 Click the Green channel.

■ The amount of green in the image is displayed.

8 Click the Blue channel.

■ The amount of blue in the image is displayed.

9 Click the RGB channel to return to the full-color image.

■ Working with channels can be useful when correcting color casts, or when masking low-contrast areas of an image.

CONVERT COLOR IMAGES TO GRAYSCALE

You can remove the color from your image by converting it to grayscale mode. This can give an image an old-fashioned look. *Grayscale* images are made up of pixels that are white, gray, and black.

CONVERT COLOR IMAGES TO GRAYSCALE

1 Click **Image**.

2 Click **Mode**.

3 Click **Grayscale**.

■ Photoshop displays an alert box.

4 Click **OK**.

■ You can click the **Don't Show Again** check box (☐ changes to ☑) to avoid the alert in the future.

How do I make just part of my image grayscale?

Define the area you would like to turn gray with a selection tool and click **Image**, **Adjustments**, and then **Desaturate**. See Chapter 4 for more about selection tools.

■ Every pixel in the image is converted to one of 256 shades of gray.

■ Gray is displayed in the image title bar.

5 Click **Window**.

6 Click **Channels**.

■ Grayscale images have a single channel (compared to an RGB image's three — see "Work in RGB Mode"), so grayscale image files take up less space than RGB images.

CREATE A DUOTONE

You can convert a grayscale image to a duotone. This is an easy way to add some color to a black-and-white photo.

A *duotone* is essentially a grayscale image with a color tint.

CREATE A DUOTONE

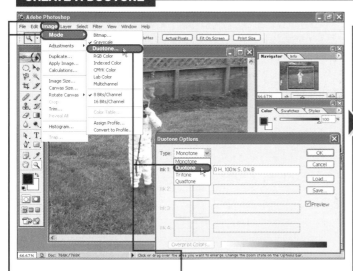

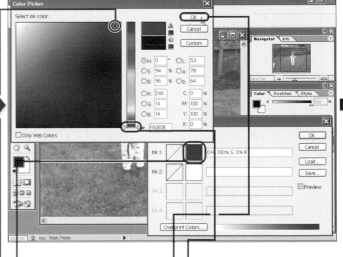

1 If necessary, convert a color image to grayscale.

Note: See "Convert Color Images to Grayscale."

2 Click **Image**.

3 Click **Mode**.

4 Click **Duotone**.

5 Click 🔽 (🔼) and click **Duotone**.

6 Click the first color swatch to open the Color Picker.

7 Click inside the window to select your first duotone color.

■ You can click and drag the slider to change the color selection. You can also enter values in the boxes to the right of the slider to define a precise color.

8 Click **OK**.

How can I use duotones?

Duotones offer a quick and
easy way to add color to a
Web page or printed
publication when all you
have available are grayscale
images.

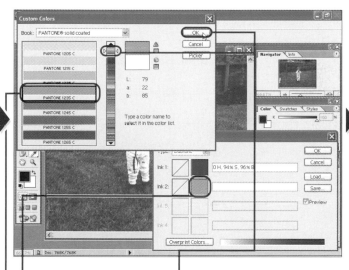

9 Click the second color
swatch to open the Custom
Colors dialog box.

10 Click inside the window
to select your second
duotone color.

■ You can click and drag the
slider to change the color
selection.

11 Click **OK**.

12 Click **OK** in the Duotone
Options dialog box.

■ Photoshop uses the two
selected colors to create the
tones in the image.

CREATE A BITMAP IMAGE

You can convert a grayscale image to a bitmap image. This can produce a photocopied effect. In Photoshop, a bitmap image is made up of only black pixels and white pixels.

The term *bitmap* is also used to describe any image made up of pixels. There is a file format called *bitmap,* abbreviated BMP, as well.

CREATE A BITMAP IMAGE

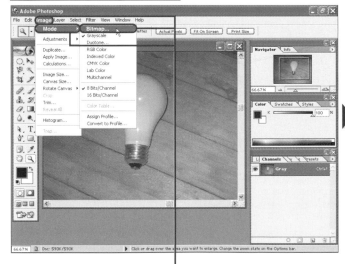

1 If you are working with a color image, convert it to grayscale.

Note: See "Convert Color Images to Grayscale."

2 Click **Image**.

3 Click **Mode**.

4 Click **Bitmap**.

5 Click ☑ (⬍) and select an option for simulating the grayscale tones with black pixels and white pixels.

6 Click **OK**.

How can I convert just part of my image to a bitmap?

Select an area of the image and click **Image**, **Adjustments**, and then **Threshold**. The selected pixels will be converted to black pixels and white pixels. You can adjust the slider in the Threshold dialog box to achieve different effects.

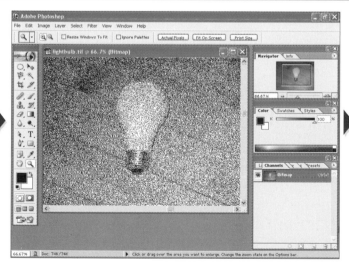

■ Photoshop converts the image to bitmap mode.

■ This figure shows the Diffusion Dither option, in which a random mixture of black pixels and white pixels simulate the grayscale tones.

■ This figure shows the 50% Threshold option, in which pixels that are less than 50% black turn to white and pixels that are more than 50% black turn to black.

CHAPTER 7

Painting and Drawing with Color

Want to add splashes, streaks, or solid areas of color to your image? Photoshop offers a variety of tools with which you can add almost any color imaginable. This chapter introduces you to those tools and shows you how to choose your colors.

SELECT FOREGROUND AND BACKGROUND COLORS

You can select two colors to work with at a time in Photoshop — a foreground color and a background color. Painting tools such as the Paintbrush apply foreground color. You apply background color when you use the Eraser tool, enlarge the image canvas, or cut pieces out of your image.

SELECT THE FOREGROUND COLOR

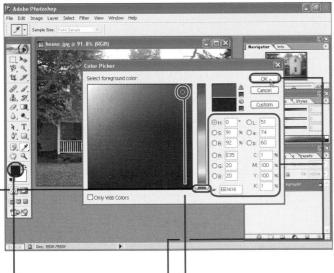

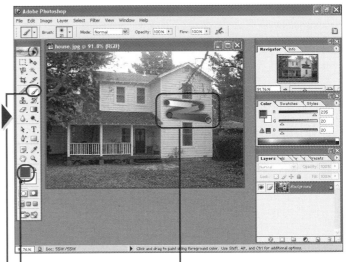

1 Click the Foreground Color box.

■ The Color Picker dialog box appears.

■ To change the range of colors that appears in the color box, click and drag the slider (▷).

2 To select a foreground color, click the color you want in the color box.

■ You can also specify a color by typing values.

3 Click **OK**.

■ The selected color appears in the Foreground Color box.

4 Click a painting tool in the toolbox.

■ This example uses the Paintbrush tool (✐).

Note: To learn more about painting tools, see the section "Using the Paintbrush Tool."

5 Click and drag to apply the color.

How do I reset the foreground and background colors?

Click the Default icon () to the lower left of the Foreground and Background icons. Doing so resets the colors to black and white.

SELECT THE BACKGROUND COLOR

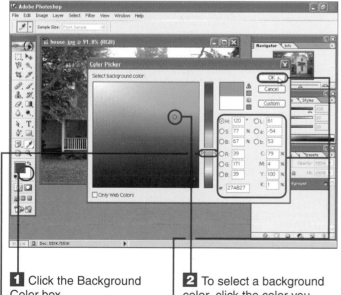

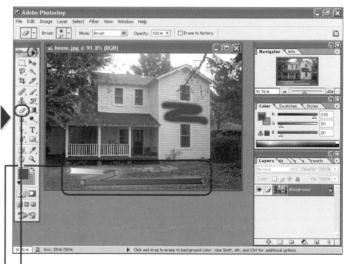

1 Click the Background Color box.

■ To change the range of colors that appears in the color box, click and drag ▷.

2 To select a background color, click the color you want in the color box.

■ You can also specify a color by typing values.

3 Click **OK**.

4 Click the Eraser tool (⌗).

5 Click and drag your mouse ○.

■ The tool "erases" by painting with the background color.

Note: Erasing occurs only in the background layer; in other layers, the eraser turns pixels transparent. See Chapter 9 for a full discussion of layers.

SELECT A WEB-SAFE COLOR

You can select one of the 216 Web-safe colors as a foreground or background color. A Web-safe color displays accurately in all Web browsers, no matter what type of monitor or operating system a user has.

See Chapter 15 for information about saving images with Web-safe colors.

SELECT A WEB-SAFE COLOR

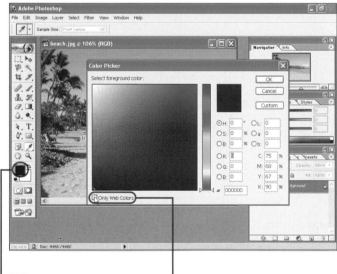

1 Click the Foreground Color box.

■ Alternatively, to select a Web-safe background color, you can click the Background Color box.

■ The Color Picker window appears.

2 Click **Only Web Colors** (☐ changes to ☑).

■ Photoshop displays only Web-safe colors in the color picker window.

3 Click a color.

■ The hex-code value for the selected color displays here.

4 Click **OK**.

■ The color appears in the Foreground Color box.

SELECT A COLOR WITH THE EYEDROPPER TOOL

You can select a color from an open image with the Eyedropper tool. The Eyedropper tool enables you to paint using a color already present in your image.

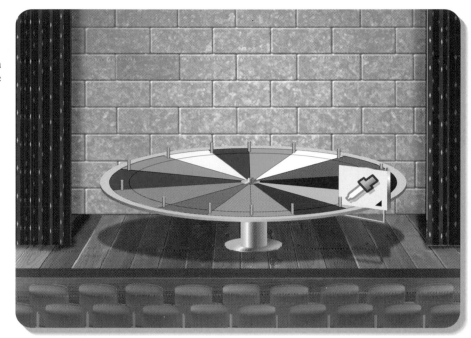

SELECT A COLOR WITH THE EYEDROPPER TOOL

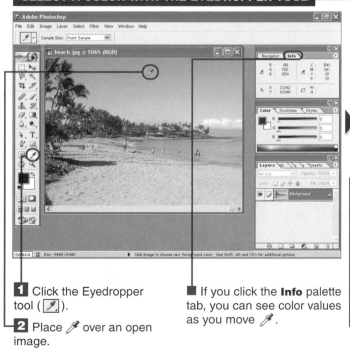

1 Click the Eyedropper tool (⧲).

2 Place ⧲ over an open image.

■ If you click the **Info** palette tab, you can see color values as you move ⧲.

3 Click to select the color of the pixel beneath ⧲'s tip.

■ The color becomes the new foreground color.

■ To select a new background color, you can press **Alt** (**option**) as you click in step **3**.

SELECT A COLOR WITH THE SWATCHES PALETTE

You can select a color with the Swatches palette. The Swatches palette lets you choose from a small set of commonly used colors.

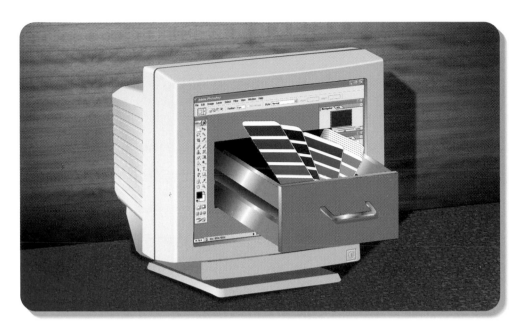

SELECT A COLOR WITH THE SWATCHES PALETTE

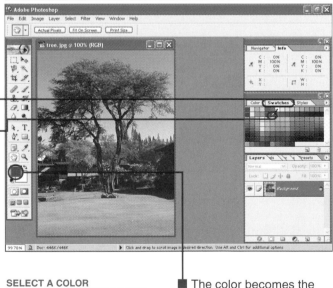

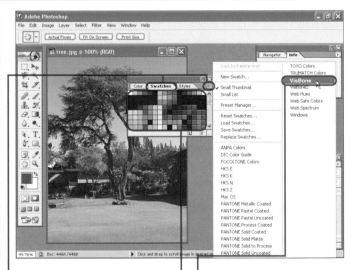

SELECT A COLOR

1 Click the **Swatches** palette tab.

2 Click a color swatch to select a foreground color.

■ The color becomes the new foreground color.

■ To select a background color, press **Alt** (**option**) as you click in step **3**.

CHANGE THE SWATCH SELECTION

1 Click the **Swatches** palette tab.

2 Click ⊙ .

3 Click a swatch set.

■ The set of swatches appears in the Swatches palette.

ADD A COLOR TO THE SWATCHES PALETTE

You can add custom colors to the Swatches palette. This enables you to easily select these colors later.

ADD A COLOR TO THE SWATCHES PALETTE

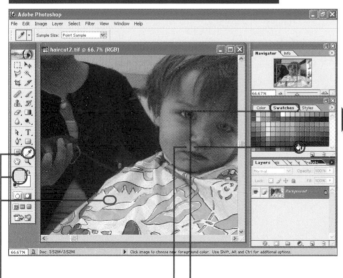

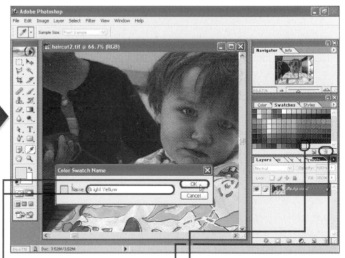

1 Click the eyedropper icon.

2 Click inside the image to select a color.

■ The color appears in the Foreground Color box.

3 Click the Swatches palette tab.

4 Place the eyedropper over an empty area of the Swatches palette (eyedropper changes to the paint bucket).

5 Click to add the color.

■ The Color Swatch Name dialog box appears.

6 Type a name for the new color swatch.

7 Click **OK**.

■ Photoshop adds the color as a new swatch.

■ You can remove a swatch by clicking it and dragging it to the trash icon.

USING THE PAINTBRUSH TOOL

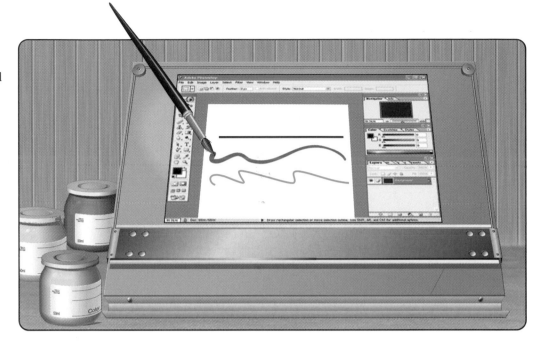

You can use the Paintbrush tool to add color to your image. You may find the paintbrush useful for applying bands of color.

To limit where the paintbrush applies color, create a selection before painting. For details, see Chapter 4.

USING THE PAINTBRUSH TOOL

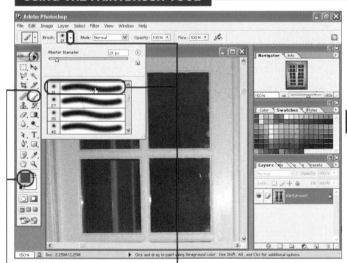

1 Click the Paintbrush tool (✐).

2 Click the Foreground Color box to select a color with which to paint.

Note: For details, see the section "Select the Foreground and Background Colors."

3 Click the Brush ⋅ and select a brush size and type.

4 Click and drag to apply the foreground color to the image.

■ To undo the most recent brush stroke, you can click **Edit** and then **Undo Paintbrush**.

Note: To undo more than one brush stroke, see Chapter 2 for more about the History palette.

What is the Airbrush tool?

You can convert your paintbrush to an airbrush by clicking the Airbrush button () in the Options bar. The Airbrush paints soft lines that get darker the longer you hold down your mouse button.

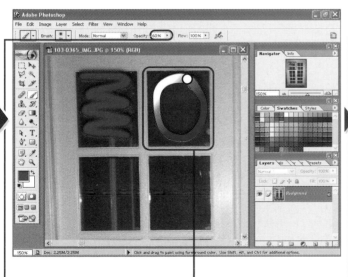

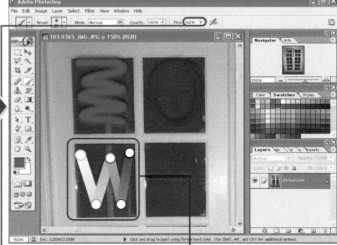

5 Type a percentage value to change the opacity of the brush strokes.

■ Alternatively, you can click the Opacity ▸ and adjust the slider.

6 Click and drag to apply the semitransparent paintbrush.

7 Type a percentage value to change how much color the brush applies.

■ Alternatively, you can click the Flow ▸ and adjust the slider.

8 Click and drag to apply the customized paintbrush.

■ Photoshop applies color per your specifications.

CHANGE BRUSH STYLES

You can select from a variety of predefined brush styles to apply color in different ways. Some of the types of brushes available include calligraphic brushes, texture brushes, and brushes that enable you to add drop shadows to objects.

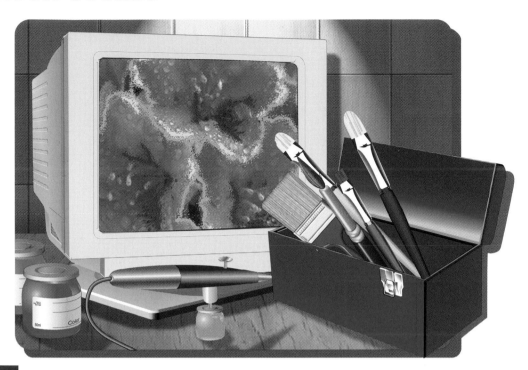

CHANGE BRUSH STYLES

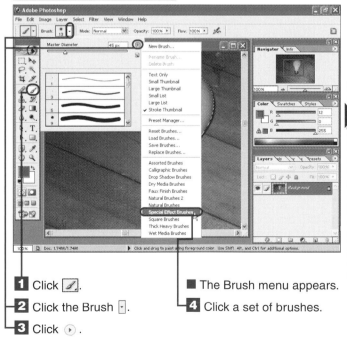

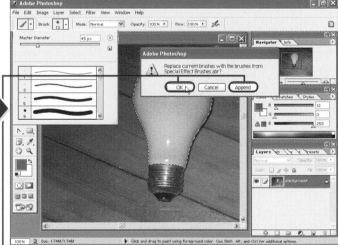

1 Click .

2 Click the Brush ▪.

3 Click ☉.

■ The Brush menu appears.

4 Click a set of brushes.

5 A dialog box appears asking if you want to replace your brushes. Click **OK**.

■ To add the set of brushes to the currently displayed set, click **Append**.

*Note: You can reset your brushes to the original set by selecting **Reset Brushes** from the Brush menu.*

How can I make a brush apply dots instead of a line?

Open the Brushes palette by clicking **Window** and then **Brushes**. Click **Brush Tip Shape**. Click and drag the spacing slider to greater than 100%. When you click and drag to apply the current brush, you get a discontiguous brush stroke.

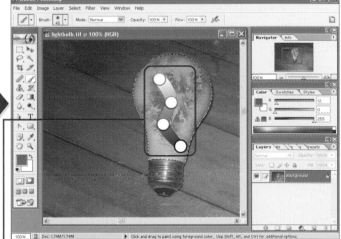

■ The new set appears in the Brush menu.

■ You can click ▾ to view all the brush styles.

6 Click a brush style to select it.

7 Click and drag to apply the new paintbrush.

■ Photoshop applies the foreground color with the brush.

■ In this example, the brush paints inside a selection, which constrains where the brush applies color.

CREATE A CUSTOM BRUSH

You can use the Brushes palette to create one-of-a-kind brushes of varying sizes and shapes. You can even specify that a brush shape that changes as it paints, to generate a random design.

CREATE A CUSTOM BRUSH

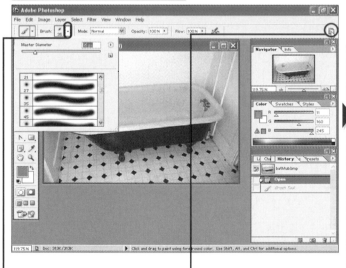

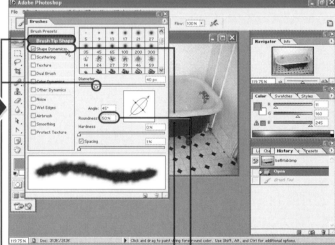

1 Click 🖌.

2 Click the Brush ⋅ and select a brush style to use as a starting point for your custom brush.

3 Click 🗐 to open the Brushes palette.

■ The Brushes palette opens.

4 Click **Brush Tip Shape**.

5 Click and drag the Diameter slider (🔺) to change the brush size.

6 Type a Roundness value between 0% and 100%. The lower the number, the more oval the brush.

■ You can adjust other settings to further define the tip shape.

7 Click **Shape Dynamics** (☐ changes to ☑).

**How do I save my custom
brush in the Brush drop-
down menu?**

Click the Brush ⊡ and then
click 🔲. A dialog box opens
allowing you to name your
custom brush. Type a name
and then click **OK** to add
your brush to the Brush
menu.

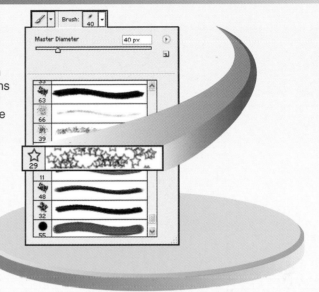

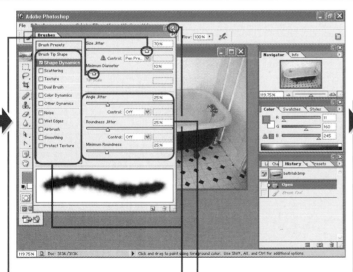

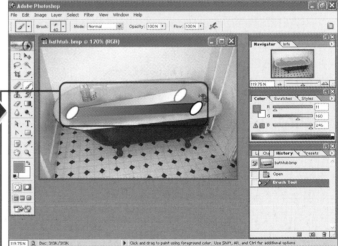

8 Click and drag the Size
Jitter slider to specify the
amount your brush will vary
in size as it paints.

9 Click and drag the
Minimum Diameter slider to
specify the smallest size the
brush will scale to when Size
Jitter is enabled.

10 Click and drag the other
sliders to control how the
brush angle and roundness
change.

■ You can click other
categories to define other
settings.

11 Click ☒ to close the
Brushes palette.

12 Click and drag to apply
the custom brush.

USING THE PENCIL TOOL

You can use the Pencil tool to draw hard-edged lines of color. Its lines are more jagged than the paintbrush's.

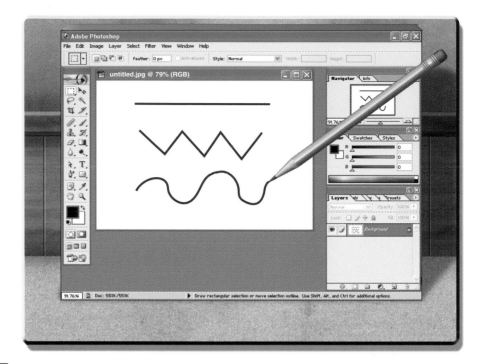

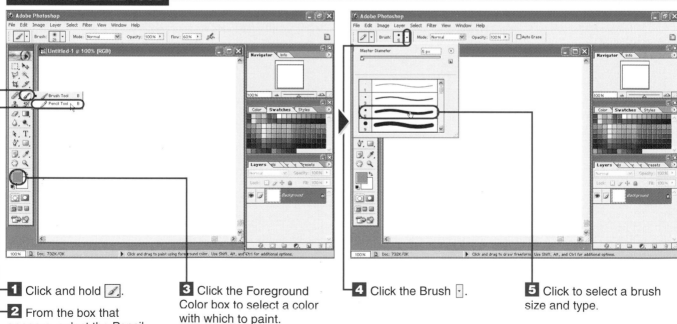

1 Click and hold (✎).

2 From the box that appears, select the Pencil tool (✎).

3 Click the Foreground Color box to select a color with which to paint.

Note: For details, see the section "Select the Foreground and Background Colors."

4 Click the Brush (·).

5 Click to select a brush size and type.

What is the Auto Erase function?

If you click **Auto Erase** (☐ changes to ☑) in the Options bar, the Pencil tool acts like an eraser when dragged over the foreground color. For more about the Eraser tool, see "Using the Eraser" in this chapter.

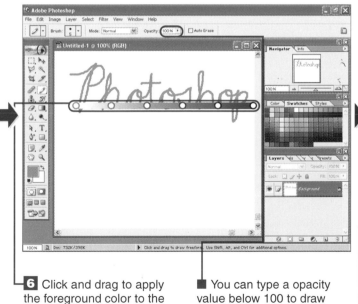

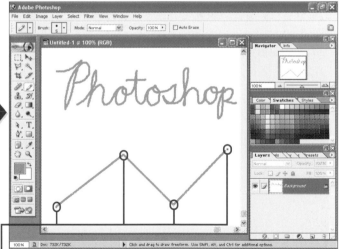

6 Click and drag to apply the foreground color to the image.

■ You can type a opacity value below 100 to draw semitransparent lines.

DRAW STRAIGHT LINES

7 Press and hold Shift.

8 Click several places inside your image, without dragging.

■ Photoshop draws straight lines between the clicked points.

APPLY A GRADIENT

You can apply a gradient, which is a transition from one color to another. This can give objects in your image a shaded or 3D look.

For another way to add a gradient to your image, see Chapter 9.

APPLY A GRADIENT

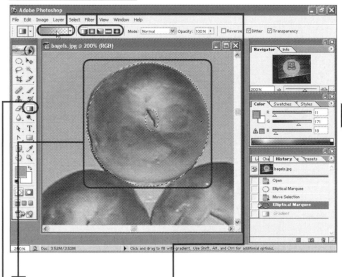

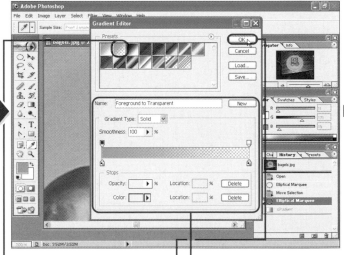

1 Make a selection.

Note: See Chapter 4 for more on making selections.

2 Click the Gradient tool (▣).

■ A linear gradient is the default. You can select different geometries in the Options bar.

3 Click the gradient swatch.

■ The Gradient Editor opens.

4 Select a preset gradient type from the top list box.

■ Photoshop shows the settings for the selected gradient below.

■ You can customize the gradient using the settings.

5 Click **OK**.

**How can I add a rainbow
gradient to my image?**

Click a rainbow swatch in the
Gradient Editor. Doing so
applies the spectrum of colors
from red to violet.

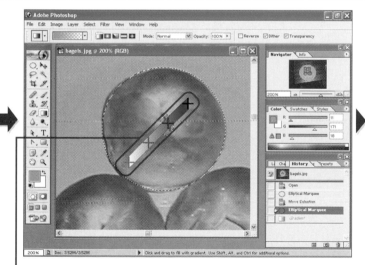

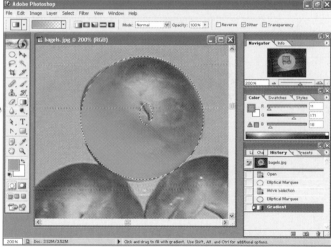

6 Click and drag inside the
selection.

*Note: This defines the direction and
transition of the gradient. Dragging a
long line with the tool produces a
gradual transition. Dragging a short
line with the tool produces an abrupt
transition.*

■ Photoshop generates a
gradient inside the selection.

USING THE PAINT BUCKET TOOL

You can fill areas in your image with solid color using the Paint Bucket tool.

The Paint Bucket tool affects only adjacent pixels in the image. You can set the Paint Bucket's Tolerance value to determine what range of colors the paint bucket affects in the image when you apply it.

To fill the pixels of a selected area, rather than just adjacent pixels, see the section "Fill a Selection."

USING THE PAINT BUCKET TOOL

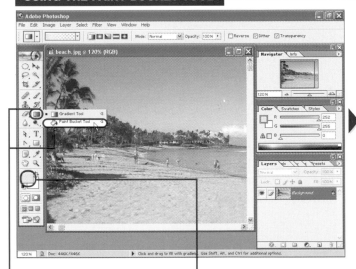

1 Click and hold ▣.

2 From the box that appears, select the Paint Bucket tool (▨).

3 Click the Foreground Color box to select a color for painting.

Note: For details, see the section "Select the Foreground and Background Colors."

4 Type a Tolerance value from 0 to 255.

■ With a low value, the tool fills only adjacent colors that are very similar to that of the clicked pixel. A high value fills a broader range of colors.

5 Click inside the image.

■ Photoshop fills an area of the image with the foreground color.

**How can I reset a tool to
its default settings?**

Right-click (Control + click)
the tool's icon on the far left
side of the Options bar and
select **Reset Tool** from the
menu that appears.

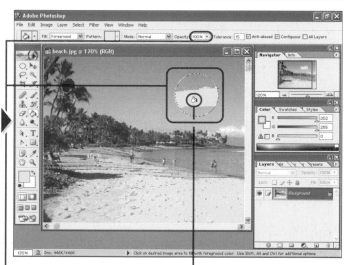

ADJUST OPACITY

6 To fill an area with a
semitransparent color, type a
percentage value of less
than 100 in the Opacity field.

7 Click inside the image.

■ Photoshop fills an area
with see-through paint.

CONSTRAIN THE COLOR

8 To constrain where you
apply the color, make a
selection before clicking.

■ In this example, the
Opacity was reset to 100%.

9 Click inside the selection.

■ The fill effect stays within
the boundary of the
selection.

FILL A SELECTION

You can fill a selection using the Fill command. The Fill command is an alternative to the Paint Bucket tool. The Fill command differs from the Paint Bucket tool in that it fills the entire selected area, not just adjacent pixels based on a tolerance value.

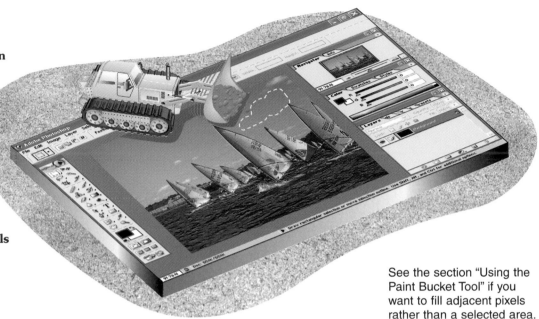

See the section "Using the Paint Bucket Tool" if you want to fill adjacent pixels rather than a selected area.

See the section "Using the Paint Bucket Tool" if you want to fill adjacent pixels rather than a selected area.

FILL A SELECTION

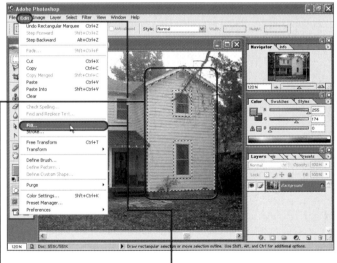

1 Define the area you want to fill using a selection tool.

Note: See Chapter 4 for more on using selection tools.

2 Click **Edit**.

3 Click **Fill**.

4 Click ▼ (⬙) and select what you want to fill with.

■ You can decrease the opacity to fill with a semi-transparent color or pattern.

5 Click **OK**.

How do I apply a "ghosted" white layer over part of an image?

Use a selection tool to define the area of the image that you want to cover. Then apply the Fill command with White selected and the Opacity set to less than 50%.

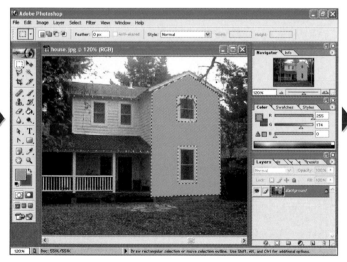

■ Photoshop fills the area.

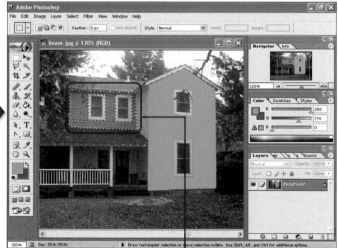

■ You can select other areas and fill them with different colors.

■ This example uses a fill with the background color set to 30% opacity.

STROKE A SELECTION

You can use the Stroke command to draw a line along the edge of a selection. This can help you highlight objects in your image.

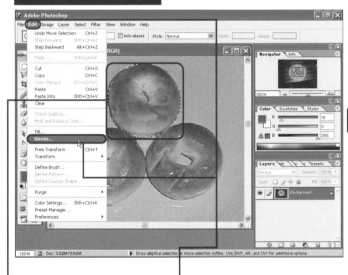

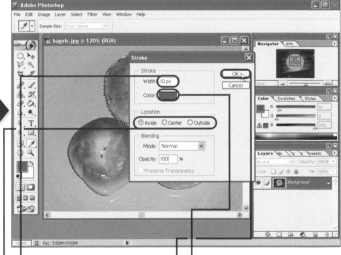

1 Select an area of the image with a selection tool.

Note: See Chapter 4 for more on using selection tools.

2 Click **Edit**.

3 Click **Stroke**.

■ The Stroke dialog box appears.

4 Type a width.

5 Click **Inside** to stroke a line on the inside of the selection, **Center** to stroke a line straddling the selection, or **Outside** to stroke a line on the outside of the selection (○ changes to ◉).

■ You can click the Color box to define the color of the stroke.

6 Click **OK**.

**How do I add a colored border to
the outside of my image?**

Click **Select** and then **All**. Then
apply the Stroke command,
clicking **Inside** as the Location.
Photoshop adds a border to the
image.

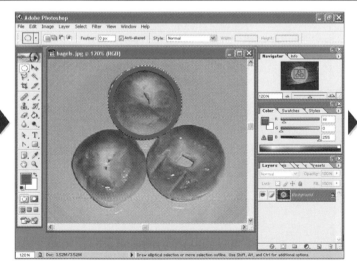

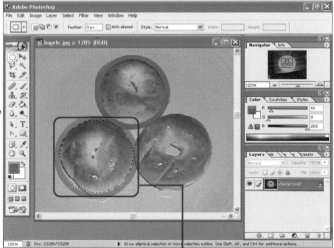

■ Photoshop strokes a line
along the selection.

■ You can select other
areas and stroke them using
different settings.

■ This stroke was applied to
the outside of the selection
at 30% opacity.

USING THE CLONE STAMP

You can clean up small flaws or erase elements in your image with the Clone Stamp tool. The tool copies information from one area of an image to another.

For other ways to correct defects in your image, see "Using the Healing Brush" and "Using the Patch Tool."

USING THE CLONE STAMP

1 Click the Clone Stamp tool (▣).

2 Click the Brush ⊡ and select a brush size and type.

3 Press and hold **Alt** (**option**) and click the area of the image from which you want to copy.

■ You do not have to select an area inside the current image; you can click another open image.

■ This example uses the tool to select an area of sky.

How can I make the clone stamp's effects look seamless?

To erase elements from your image with the clone stamp without leaving a trace, try the following:

■ Clone between areas of similar color and texture.

■ To apply the clone stamp more subtly, lower its opacity.

■ Use a soft-edged brush shape.

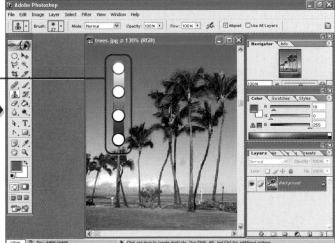

4 Release the **Alt** (**option**) key.

5 Click and drag inside the selection to apply the clone stamp.

■ Photoshop copies the previously clicked area to where you click and drag.

6 Click and drag repeatedly over the image to achieve the desired effect.

■ As you apply the tool, you can press **Alt** (**option**) and click again to select a different area from which to copy.

■ This example uses a selection of the sky to eliminate part of a tree in the image.

USING THE PATTERN STAMP

You can paint with a pattern using the Pattern Stamp tool. The tool gives you a free-form way to add repeating elements to your images.

USING THE PATTERN STAMP

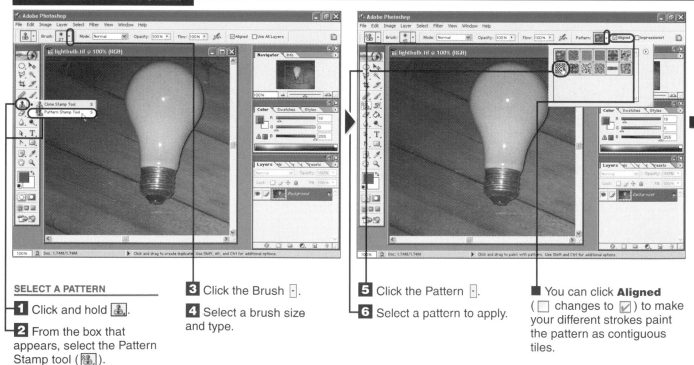

SELECT A PATTERN

1 Click and hold 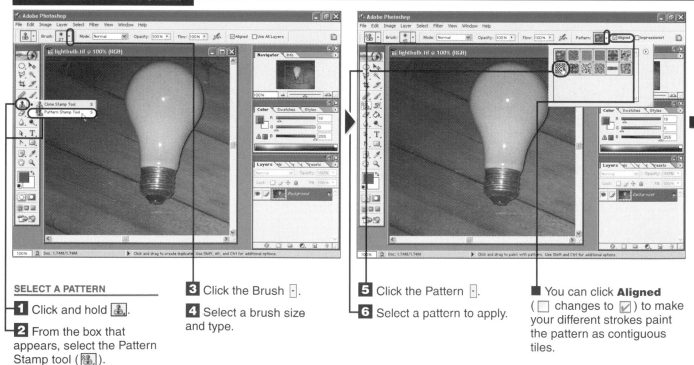.

2 From the box that appears, select the Pattern Stamp tool ( ).

3 Click the Brush ·.

4 Select a brush size and type.

5 Click the Pattern ·.

6 Select a pattern to apply.

■ You can click **Aligned** (☐ changes to ☑) to make your different strokes paint the pattern as contiguous tiles.

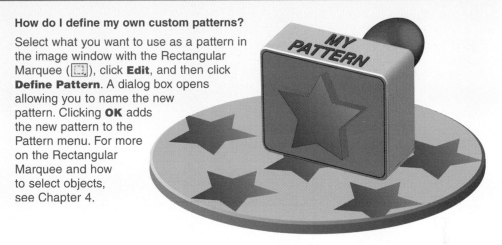

How do I define my own custom patterns?

Select what you want to use as a pattern in the image window with the Rectangular Marquee (□), click **Edit**, and then click **Define Pattern**. A dialog box opens allowing you to name the new pattern. Clicking **OK** adds the new pattern to the Pattern menu. For more on the Rectangular Marquee and how to select objects, see Chapter 4.

7 Click and drag inside the selection to apply the pattern.

■ The pattern applies to where you click and drag.

APPLY A DIFFERENT OPACITY

8 Type a value of less than 100 in the Opacity box.

9 Click and drag inside the selection to apply the pattern.

■ Decreasing the opacity applies a semi-transparent pattern.

USING THE HEALING BRUSH

You can correct defects in your image using the Healing Brush. The Healing Brush is similar to the Clone Stamp in that it copies pixels from one area of the image to another. However, the Healing Brush takes into account the texture and lighting of the image as it works, which can make its modifications more convincing.

USING THE HEALING BRUSH

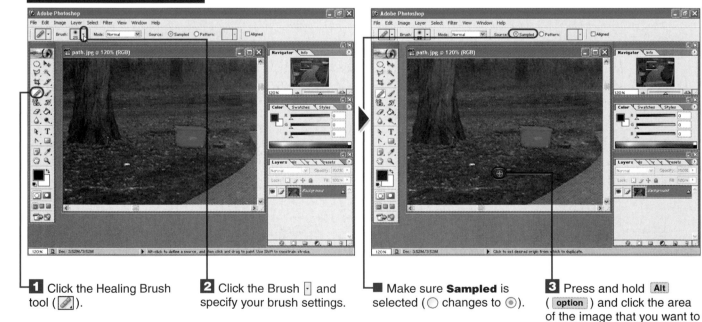

1 Click the Healing Brush tool ( ).

2 Click the Brush and specify your brush settings.

■ Make sure **Sampled** is selected (○ changes to ⊙).

3 Press and hold Alt (option) and click the area of the image that you want to heal with.

What does the Healing Brush's Pattern option do?

It allows you to correct defects in your image by painting over them with a predefined pattern. This can be useful if you want to apply a specific texture over defects, rather than with pixels cloned from somewhere in the image.

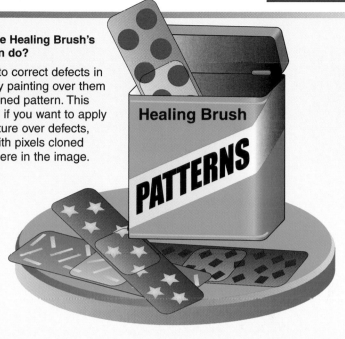

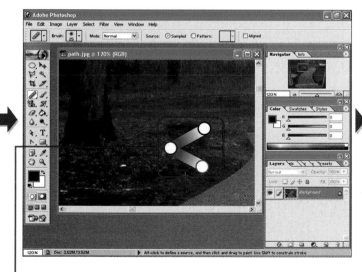

4 Release the Alt (option) key.

5 Click and drag inside the selection to apply the healing stamp.

■ Photoshop copies the selected area to where you click and drag.

6 Stop dragging and release the mouse button.

■ Photoshop adjusts the copied pixels to account for the lighting and texture present in the image.

USING THE PATCH TOOL

The Patch tool lets you correct defects in your image by selecting them and dragging the selection to an unflawed area of your image. This can be useful if there is a large part of your image that is without flaws.

For other ways to correct defects in your image, see "Using the Clone Stamp" and "Using the Healing Brush."

USING THE PATCH TOOL

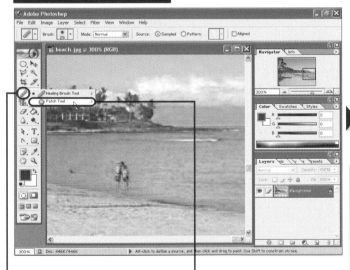

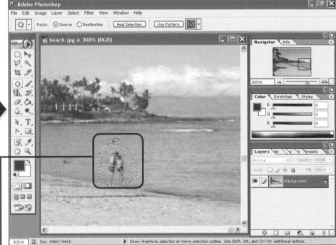

1 Click the Healing Brush tool (pencil icon).

2 From the box that appears, click the Patch tool (patch icon).

3 Click and drag to select the part of your image that contains the defects that you want to patch.

■ When making selections, the Patch tool works similarly to the Lasso tool. See Chapter 4 for more about the Lasso tool.

How does the Patch tool determine what are defects in my selection?

It does it by comparing what color and texture is the same in the two selections, and what color and texture is different. The tool then tries to eliminate the differences — the defects — while retaining the overall color and texture.

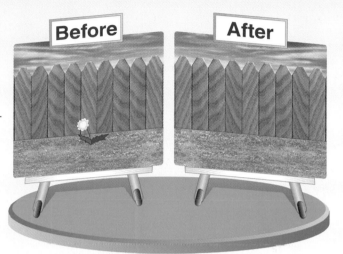

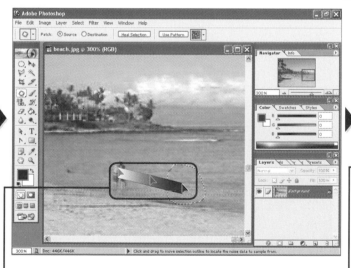

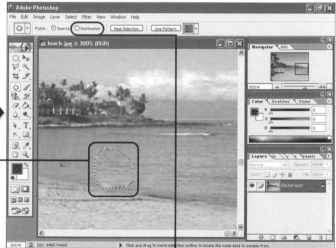

4 Click inside the selection and drag it to an area that does not have defects.

■ Photoshop uses pixels from the destination selection to patch the defects in the source selection.

■ You can click **Destination** (○ changes to ◉) to patch defects in the reverse order — flaws in the destination selection are corrected with the pixels from the source selection.

USING THE HISTORY BRUSH

You can use the History brush to paint a previous state of your image from the History palette into the current image. This can be useful if you want to revert just a part of your image.

USING THE HISTORY BRUSH

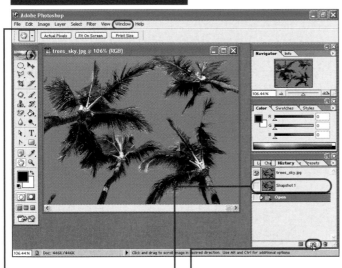

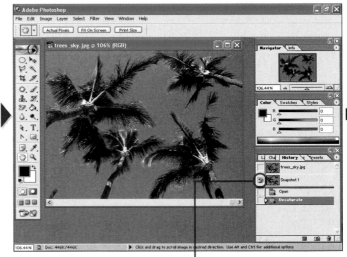

1 Click **Window**.

2 Click **History**.

■ The History palette opens.

3 Click the New Snapshot button (📷) in the History palette.

■ Photoshop puts a copy of the current state of the image into the History palette.

4 Modify your image to make it different from the newly created snapshot.

■ In this example, the image was desaturated.

5 Click to the left side of the snapshot to select it as the History brush source.

How do I paint onto a blank image with the History brush?

Start with a photographic image, take a snapshot of it with the New Snapshot button (), and then fill the image with a solid color. See "Fill a Selection" for details. You can then use the History brush ([🖌]) to paint in the photographic content.

6 Click the History brush ([🖌]).

7 Click and drag inside the image.

■ Pixels from the previous snapshot are painted into the image.

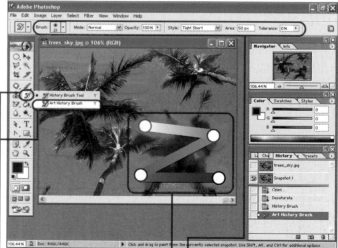

USING THE ART HISTORY BRUSH

1 Click and hold [🖌] and select the Art History brush ([🖌]).

■ The Art History brush lets you paint in snapshot information with an added impressionistic effect.

2 Specify the settings for the brush.

3 Click and drag to apply an artistic effect.

USING THE ERASER

You can delete elements from your images using the Eraser tool. This can be useful when you are trying to separate elements from their backgrounds.

USING THE ERASER

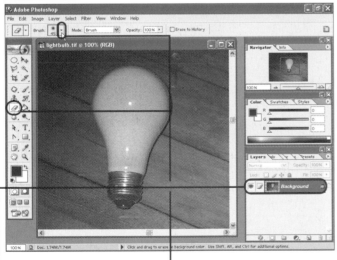

IN THE BACKGROUND LAYER

1 Click the Background layer in the Layers palette.

■ If you start with a newly scanned image, the background layer is the only layer.

Note: See Chapter 9 for more on layers.

2 Click the Eraser tool (⟋).

3 Click the Brush ⬚ and select a brush size and type.

4 Click and drag inside the image.

■ Photoshop erases the image by painting with the background color.

How can I erase areas of similar color in my image quickly?

If you click and hold  in the toolbox, a box appears allowing you to select the Background Eraser ( ) or the Magic Eraser ( ). The Background Eraser works by sampling the pixel color beneath the center of the brush, and erasing similar colors that are underneath the brush. The Magic Eraser also samples the color beneath the cursor but erases similar pixels throughout the layer. You can adjust the Tolerance of both tools to control how much they erase.

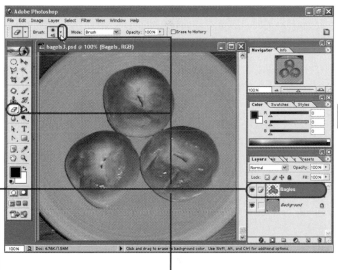

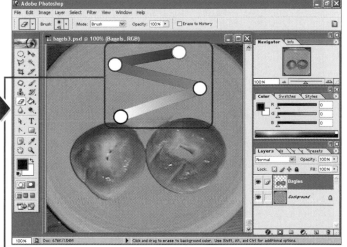

IN A REGULAR LAYER

1 Click a nonbackground layer in the Layers palette.

Note: See Chapter 9 for more on layers.

2 Click the Eraser tool ( ).

3 Click the Brush and select a brush size and type.

4 Click and drag inside the image.

■ Photoshop erases elements in the layer by making pixels transparent.

CHAPTER 8

Adjusting Colors

Do you want to fine-tune the colors in your image — darken them, lighten them, or remove them completely? This chapter introduces the tools that let you do the trick.

CHANGE BRIGHTNESS AND CONTRAST

**The Brightness/
Contrast command
provides a simple
way to make
adjustments to the
highlights and
shadows of your
image.**

To change the
brightness or
contrast of small
parts of your image,
use the Dodge or
Burn tool. See "Using
the Dodge and Burn
Tools," in this chapter,
for details.

If you make a selection
before performing the
Brightness/Contrast
command, changes
affect only the selected
pixels. Similarly, if you
have a multilayered
image, your
adjustments affect only
the selected layer. See
Chapter 4 to learn how
to make a selection,
and Chapter 9 for
more on layers.

CHANGE BRIGHTNESS AND CONTRAST

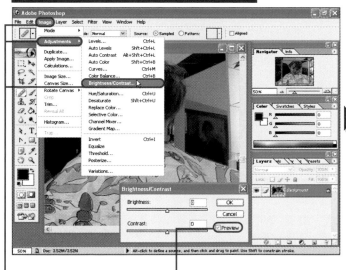

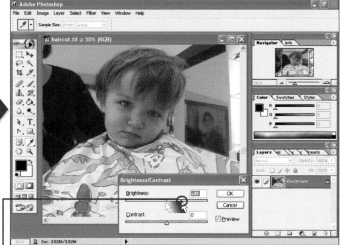

1 Click **Image**.

2 Click **Adjustments**.

3 Click
Brightness/Contrast.

■ The Brightness/Contrast
dialog box appears with
sliders set to 0.

4 To display your
adjustments in the
image window as you
make them,
click **Preview** (☐ changes
to ☑).

5 Click and drag the
Brightness slider (△).

■ Drag △ to the right to
lighten the image, or to the
left to darken the image.

■ You can also lighten the
image by typing a number
from 1 to 100, or darken the
image by typing a negative
number from –1 to –100.

How can I adjust the contrast of an image automatically?

Click **Image**, **Adjustments**, and then **Auto Contrast**. Photoshop converts the very lightest pixels in the image to white and the very darkest pixels in the image to black. Making the highlights brighter and the shadows darker boosts the contrast, which can improve the appearance of poorly exposed photographs.

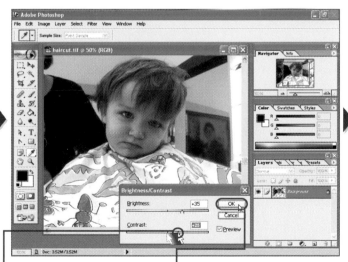

6 Click and drag the Contrast slider (△).

■ Drag △ to the right to increase the contrast, or to the left to decrease the contrast.

Note: Increasing contrast can bring out details in your image. Decreasing it can soften the details.

■ You can also increase the contrast by typing a number from 1 to 100, or decrease the contrast by typing a negative number from –1 to –100.

7 Click **OK**.

■ Photoshop applies the new brightness and contrast values.

USING THE DODGE AND BURN TOOLS

You can use the Dodge and Burn tools to brighten or darken a specific area of an image, respectively.

Dodge is a photographic term that describes the diffusing of light when developing a film negative. *Burn* is a photographic term that describes the focusing of light when developing a film negative.

These tools are an alternative to the Brightness/Contrast command, which affects the entire image. To brighten or darken the entire image, see the section "Change Brightness and Contrast."

USING THE DODGE TOOL

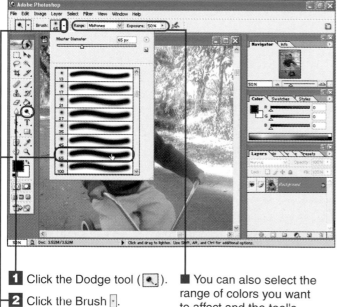

1 Click the Dodge tool ().

2 Click the Brush ⊡.

3 Click the brush that you want to use.

■ You can also select the range of colors you want to affect and the tool's exposure, or strength.

4 Click and drag over the area that you want to lighten.

■ Photoshop lightens the area.

How do I invert the bright and dark colors in an image?

Click **Image**, **Adjustments**, and then **Invert**. This makes the image look like a film negative. Bright colors become dark, and vice versa.

USING THE BURN TOOL

1 Click and hold the Dodge tool ().

2 Click the Burn tool (🖌) in the box that appears.

■ You can select the brush, the range of colors you want to affect, and the tool's exposure, or strength.

3 Click and drag over the area that you want to darken.

■ Photoshop darkens the area.

USING THE BLUR AND SHARPEN TOOLS

You can sharpen or blur specific areas of your image with the Blur and Sharpen tools. This allows you to emphasize or de-emphasize objects in a photo.

You can blur or sharpen the entire image by using one of the Blur or Sharpen commands located in Photoshop's Filter menu. See Chapter 11 for more information.

USING THE BLUR TOOL

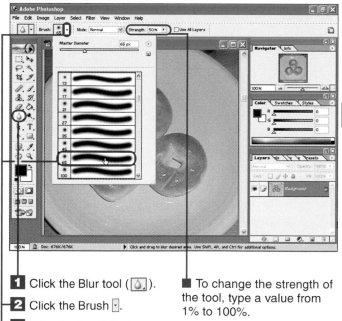

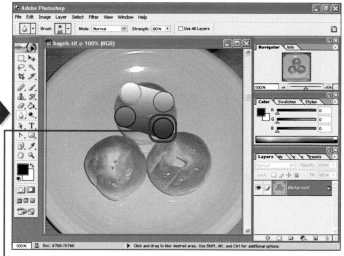

1 Click the Blur tool ().

2 Click the Brush ▪.

3 Click the brush that you want to use.

■ To change the strength of the tool, type a value from 1% to 100%.

4 Click and drag to blur an area of the image.

What is the Smudge tool?

The Smudge tool () is another tool in the Photoshop toolbox. It simulates dragging a finger through wet paint, shifting colors and blurring your image. You can access it by clicking and holding the tool.

USING THE SHARPEN TOOL

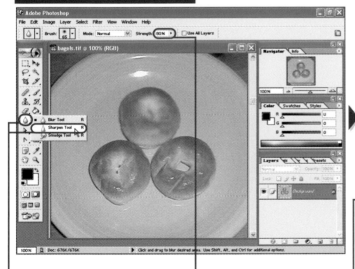

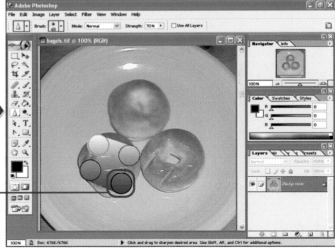

1 Click and hold the Blur tool.

2 Click the Sharpen tool in the box that appears.

■ Type a value from 1% to 100% to set the strength of the tool.

3 Click and drag to sharpen an area of the image.

ADJUST LEVELS

The Levels command lets you make fine adjustments to the highlights, midtones, or shadows of an image.

Although more difficult to use, the Levels command offers more control over brightness than the Brightness/Contrast command covered in the section "Change Brightness and Contrast."

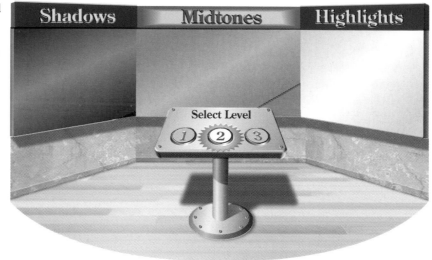

To affect only selected pixels, select them before performing the Levels command. Similarly, if you have a multilayered image, your adjustments affect only the selected layer. See Chapter 4 to learn how to make a selection, and Chapter 9 for more on layers.

ADJUST LEVELS

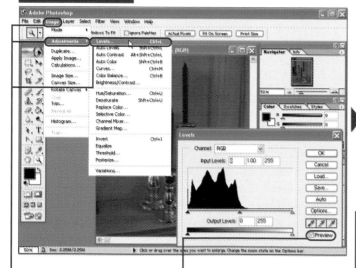

1 Click **Image**.

2 Click **Adjustments**.

3 Click **Levels**.

■ The Levels dialog box appears.

4 To display your adjustments in the image window as you make them, click **Preview** (☐ changes to ☑).

■ Use the Input sliders to adjust an image's brightness, midtones, and highlights.

5 Click and drag ▲ to the right to darken shadows and increase contrast.

6 Click and drag ▲ to the left to lighten the bright areas of the image and increase contrast.

7 Click and drag ▲ to adjust the midtones of the image.

**How do you adjust the brightness
levels of an image automatically?**

Click **Image**, **Adjustments**, and
then **Auto Levels**. Photoshop
converts the very lightest pixels in
the image to white and the very
darkest pixels in the image to
black. This command is similar to
the Auto Contrast command and
can quickly improve the contrast
of an overly gray photographic
image. See the section
"Change Brightness and
Contrast" for more
information.

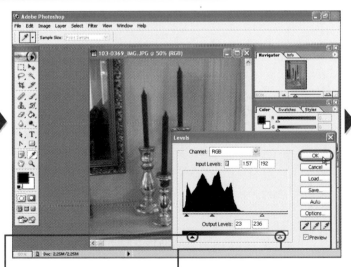

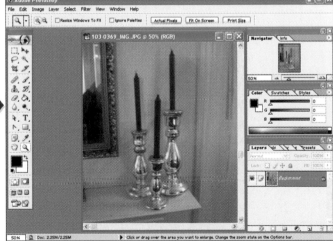

■ The Output sliders let you
decrease the contrast while
either lightening or darkening
the image.

8 Click and drag ▲ to the
right to lighten the image.

9 Click and drag △ to
the left to darken the image.

10 Click **OK**.

■ Photoshop makes
brightness and contrast
adjustments to the image.

ADJUST HUE AND SATURATION

You can change the hue to shift the component colors of an image. You can change the saturation to adjust the color intensity in an image.

If you make a selection before performing the Hue/Saturation command, you affect only the selected pixels. Similarly, if you have a multilayered image, your adjustments affect only the selected layer. See Chapter 4 to learn how to make a selection, and Chapter 9 for more on layers.

ADJUST HUE AND SATURATION

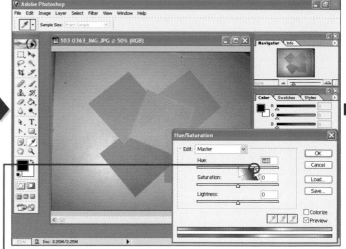

1 Click **Image**.

2 Click **Adjustments**.

3 Click **Hue/Saturation**.

■ The Hue/Saturation dialog box appears.

4 To display your adjustments in the image window as you make them, click **Preview** (☐ changes to ☑).

5 Click and drag the Hue slider (🛆) to shift the colors in the image. See the tip on the next page for details.

■ Dragging 🛆 left or right shifts the colors in different, and sometimes bizarre, ways.

■ In this example, adjusting the hue has changed the orange square to yellow.

How does the adjustment of an image's hues work?

When you adjust an image's hues in Photoshop, its colors shift according to their position on the color wheel. The color wheel is a graphical way of presenting all the colors in the visible spectrum.

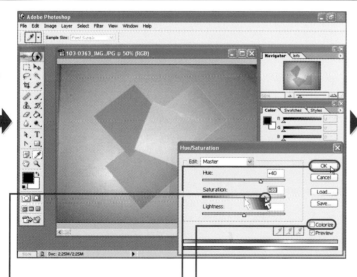

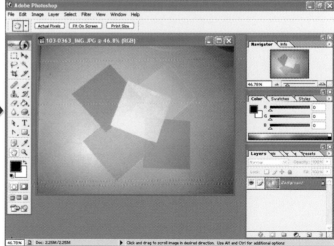

6 Click and drag the Saturation slider (⬦).

■ Dragging ⬦ to the right or to the left increases or decreases the intensity of the image's colors, respectively.

■ Clicking **Colorize** (☐ changes to ☑), turns the image — even a grayscale one — into a monotone, or one-color, image. You can adjust the color with the sliders.

7 Click **OK**.

■ Photoshop makes the color adjustments to the image.

USING THE SPONGE TOOL

You can use the Sponge tool to adjust the color saturation, or color intensity, of a specific area of an image. This can help bring out the colors in washed-out areas of photos.

USING THE SPONGE TOOL

DECREASE SATURATION

1 Click and hold the Dodge tool (⬛).

2 Click the Sponge tool (⬛) in the box that appears.

3 Click the Brush ⬝ and select the brush that you want to use.

4 Click ⬝ (⬝) and select **Desaturate**.

5 Click and drag the mouse ◯ to decrease the saturation of an area of the image.

146

How can I easily convert a color image to grayscale?

Click **Image**, **Adjustments**, and then **Desaturate**. This command effectively sets the saturation value of the image to 0, converting it to grayscale.

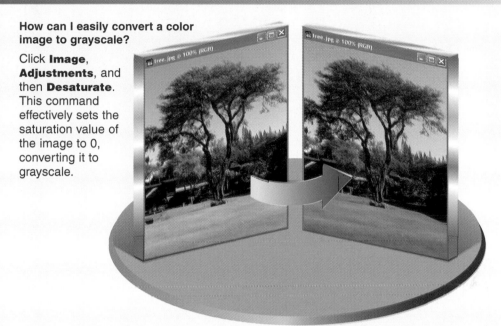

INCREASE SATURATION

1 Perform steps **1** through **3** on the previous page.

2 Click ⬇ (◆) and select **Saturate**.

3 Click and drag the mouse ◯ to increase the saturation of an area of the image.

■ You can adjust the strength of the Sponge tool by changing the Flow setting from 1% to 100%.

ADJUST COLOR BALANCE

You can use the Color Balance command to change the amounts of specific colors in your image. This can be useful if you need to remove a color cast introduced by a scanner or by age.

If you make a selection before performing the Color Balance command, you affect only the selected pixels. Similarly, if you have a multilayered image, your adjustments affect only the selected layer. See Chapter 4 to learn how to make a selection, and Chapter 9 for more on layers.

ADJUST COLOR BALANCE

1 Click **Image**.

2 Click **Adjustments**.

3 Click **Color Balance**.

■ The Color Balance dialog box appears.

4 To display your adjustments in the image window as you make them, click **Preview** (☐ changes to ☑).

5 Select the tones in the image that you want to affect (○ changes to ◉).

6 Click and drag a color slider (△) toward the color you want to add more of.

■ To add a warm cast to your image, you can drag a slider toward red or magenta. To add a cool cast, you can drag a slider toward blue or cyan.

How do I change the color of an object in my image?

Select the object with a selection tool and then apply the Color Balance command.

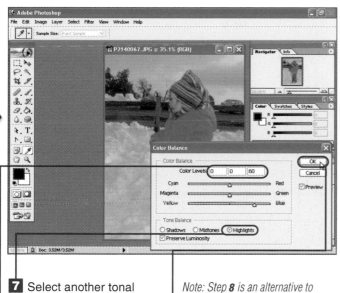

7 Select another tonal range.

8 Type a number from –100 to 100 in a color level field.

*Note: Step **8** is an alternative to dragging a slider.*

9 Click **OK**.

■ Photoshop makes color adjustments to the image.

Note: If you make a selection before performing the Color Balance command, only the selected pixels are affected. Similarly, if your image is multilayered, only the selected layer is affected.

USING THE VARIATIONS COMMAND

The Variations command gives you a user-friendly interface with which to perform color adjustments in your image.

If you make a selection before performing the Variations command, you affect only the selected pixels. Similarly, if you have a multilayered image, your adjustments affect only the selected layer. See Chapter 4 to learn how to make a selection, and Chapter 9 for more on layers.

USING THE VARIATIONS COMMAND

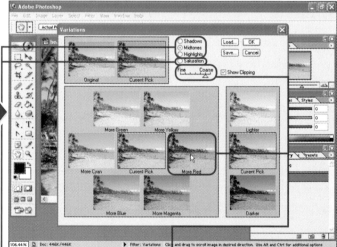

1 Click **Image**.

2 Click **Adjustments**.

3 Click **Variations**.

■ The Variations dialog box appears.

4 Select a tonal range of your image to adjust (○ changes to ◉).

■ Alternatively, you can select **Saturation**, or strength of color (○ changes to ◉).

5 Click and drag ▲ left to perform small adjustments, or right to make large adjustments.

6 To add a color to your image, click one of the More thumbnails.

How can I undo color adjustments while using the Variations dialog box?

If you clicked one of the More thumbnail images to increase a color, you can click the More thumbnail image opposite to undo the effect. When you add colors in equal amounts to an image, the colors opposite one another — for example, red and cyan — cancel each other out. Note that clicking the **Original** image in the upper-left corner returns the image to its original state as well.

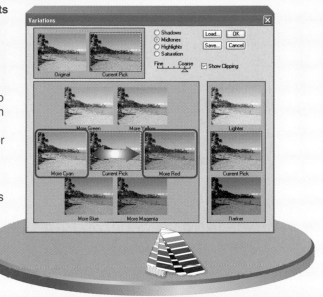

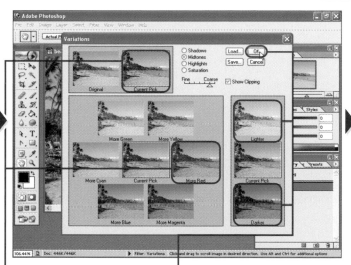

■ The result of the adjustment shows up in the Current Pick thumbnail.

■ To increase the effect, you can click the More thumbnail again.

■ You can decrease the brightness of the image by clicking **Darker**.

■ You can increase the brightness by clicking **Lighter**.

7 Click **OK**.

■ Photoshop makes the color adjustments to the image.

CHAPTER 9

Working with Layers

Do you want to separate the elements in your image so that you can move and transform them independently of one another? You can do this by placing them in different layers.

WHAT ARE LAYERS?

A Photoshop image can consist of multiple layers, with each layer containing different objects in the image.

Layer Independence

Layered Photoshop files act like several images combined into one. Each layer of an image has its own set of pixels that you can move and transform independently of the pixels in other layers.

Apply Commands to Layers

Most Photoshop commands affect only the layer that you select. For example, if you click and drag using the Move tool, the selected layer moves while the other layers stay in place; if you apply a color adjustment, only colors in the selected layer change.

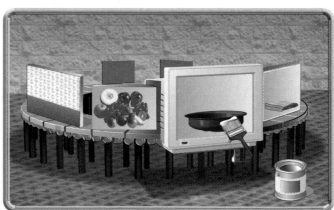

Manipulate Layers

You can combine, duplicate, and hide layers in an image. You can also shuffle the order in which layers are stacked.

Transparency

Layers can have transparent areas, where the elements on the layers below can show through. When you perform a cut or erase command on a layer, the affected pixels become transparent.

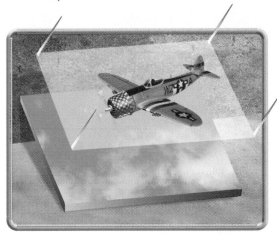

Adjustment Layers

Adjustment layers are special layers that contain information about color or tonal adjustments. An adjustment layer affects the pixels in all the layers below it. You can increase or decrease an adjustment layer's strength to get precisely the effect you want.

Save Layered Files

You can only save multilayered images in the Photoshop and TIFF file formats. To save a layered image in another file format — for example, PICT, GIF, BMP, or JPEG — you must combine the image's layers into a single layer, a process known as *flattening*. For more information about saving files, see Chapter 15.

CREATE AND ADD TO A LAYER

To keep elements in your image independent from one another, you can create separate layers and add objects to them.

CREATE A LAYER

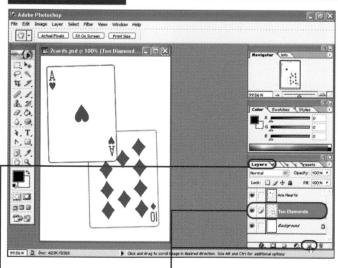

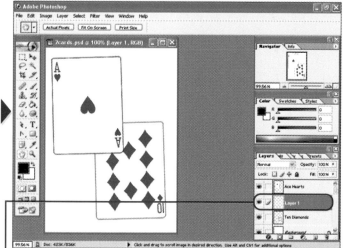

1 Click the **Layers** tab to select the Layers palette.

■ If the Layers tab is hidden, you can click **Window** and then **Layers** to open the Layers palette.

2 Click the layer above which you want to add the new layer.

3 In the Layers palette, click the New Layer button (▣).

■ Alternatively, you can click **Layer**, **New**, and then **Layer**.

■ Photoshop creates a new, transparent layer.

Note: To change the name of a layer, see the section "Rename a Layer."

What is the Background layer?

The Background layer is the default bottom layer that appears when you create a new image or when you import an image from a scanner. You can create new layers on top of a Background layer, but not below it. Unlike other layers, a Background layer cannot contain transparent pixels.

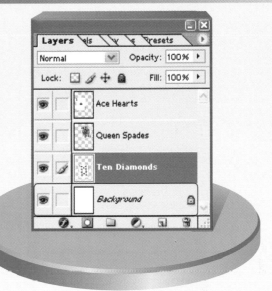

COPY AND PASTE INTO A LAYER

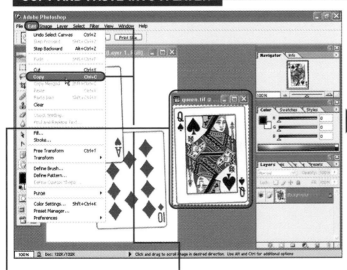

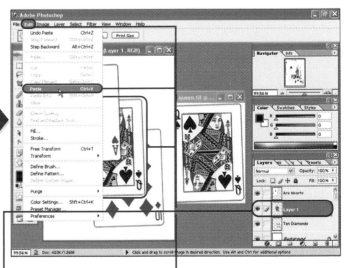

Note: This example shows adding content to the new layer by copying and pasting from another image file.

1 Open another image.

2 Using a selection tool, select the content you want to copy in the other image.

Note: See Chapter 1 for more about opening an image. See Chapter 4 for more about the selection tools.

3 Click **Edit**.

4 Click **Copy**.

5 Click the image window where you created the new layer.

6 Click the new layer in the Layers palette.

7 Click **Edit**.

8 Click **Paste**.

■ The selected content from the other image pastes into the new layer.

HIDE A LAYER

You can hide a layer to temporarily remove elements in that layer from view.

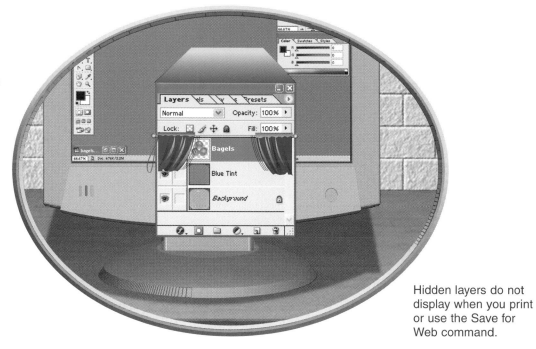

Hidden layers do not display when you print or use the Save for Web command.

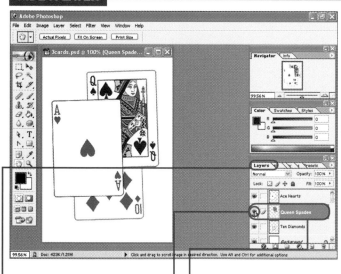

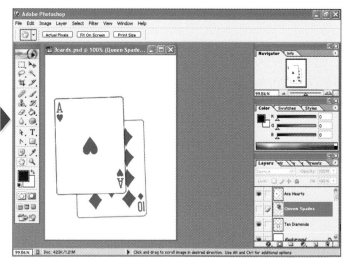

1 Click the **Layers** tab to select the Layers palette.

■ If the Layers tab is hidden, you can click **Window** and then **Layers** to open the Layers palette.

2 Click a layer.

3 Click the Eye icon (👁) for the layer. The icon disappears.

■ Photoshop hides the layer.

■ To show one layer and hide all the others, you can press `Alt` (`option`) and click the 👁 for the layer.

Note: You can also delete a layer. See the section "Delete a Layer" for more information.

You can use the Move
tool to reposition the
elements in one layer
without moving those
in others.

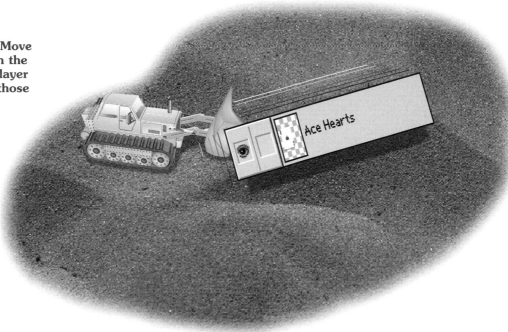

MOVE A LAYER

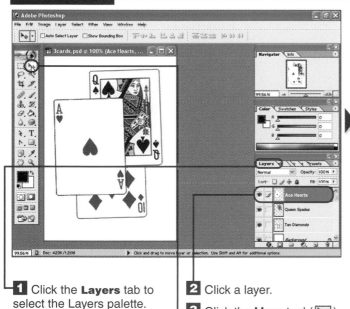

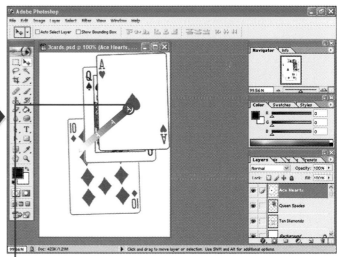

1 Click the **Layers** tab to
select the Layers palette.

■ If the Layers tab is hidden,
you can click **Window** and
then **Layers** to open the
palette.

2 Click a layer.

3 Click the Move tool ().

4 Click and drag inside the
window.

■ Content in the selected
layer moves.

■ Content in the other layers
does not move.

*Note: To move several layers at
once, see the section "Link Layers."*

DUPLICATE A LAYER

By duplicating a layer,
you can manipulate
elements in an image
while keeping a copy of
their original state.

DUPLICATE A LAYER

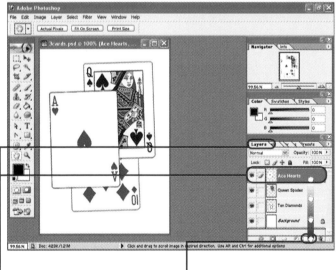

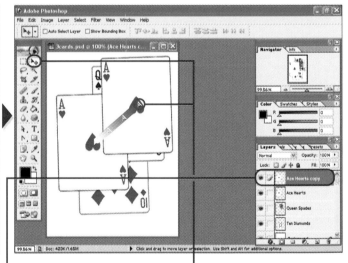

1 Click the **Layers** tab to select the Layers palette.

■ If the Layers tab is hidden, you can click **Window** and then **Layers** to open the Layers palette.

2 Click a layer.

3 Click and drag the layer to .

■ Alternatively, you can click **Layer** and then **Duplicate Layer**, in which case a dialog box appears allowing you to name the layer.

■ Photoshop duplicates the selected layer.

Note: To rename the duplicate layer, see "Rename a Layer."

■ You can see that Photoshop has duplicated the layer by selecting the new layer, clicking, and clicking and dragging the layer.

You can delete a layer
when you no longer have
a use for its contents.

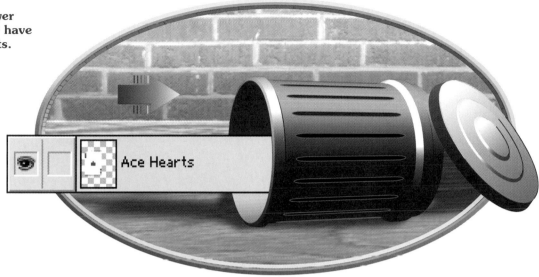

DELETE A LAYER

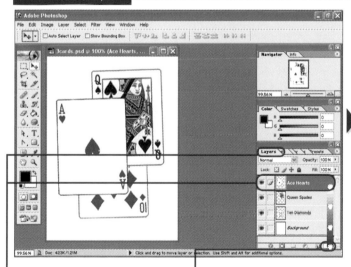

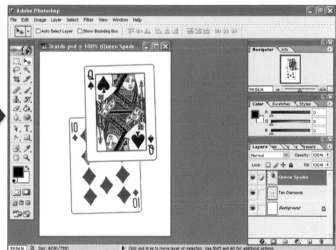

1 Click the **Layers** tab to
select the Layers palette.

2 Click a layer.

3 Click and drag the layer
to 🗑.

■ Alternatively, you can
click **Layer** and then **Delete
Layer**, in which case a
confirmation dialog box
appears.

■ Photoshop deletes
the selected layer, and
the content in the layer
disappears from the image
window.

*Note: You can also hide a layer. See
the section "Hide a Layer" for more
information.*

REORDER LAYERS

You can change the
stacking order of layers
to move elements
forward or backward in
your image.

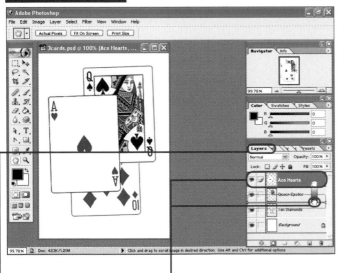

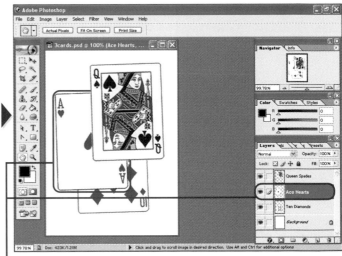

USING THE LAYERS PALETTE

1 Click the **Layers** tab to
select the Layers palette.

■ If the Layers tab is hidden,
you can click **Window** and
then **Layers** to open the
palette.

2 Click a layer.

3 Click and drag the layer
to change its arrangement in
the stack.

■ The layer assumes its new
position in the stack.

Are there shortcuts for changing the order of layers?

You can shift a layer forward one step in the stack by pressing Ctrl +] (⌘ +]). You can shift a layer backward by pressing Ctrl + [(⌘ + [). Pressing Shift + Ctrl +] (Shift + ⌘ +]) or Shift + Ctrl + [(Shift + ⌘ + [) will move a layer to the very front or very back of the stack, respectively.

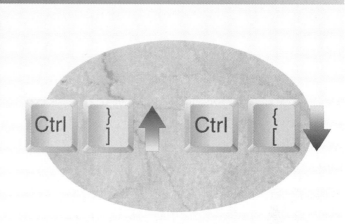

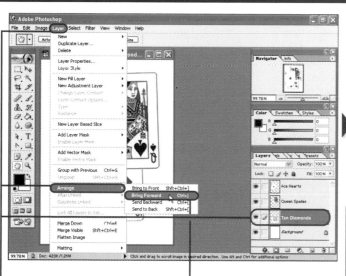

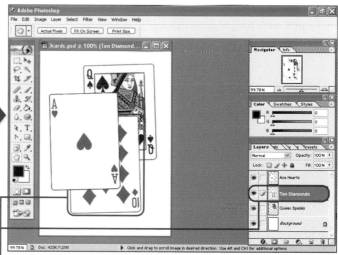

USING THE ARRANGE COMMANDS

1 Click a layer.

2 Click **Layer**.

3 Click **Arrange**.

4 Click the command for how you would like to move the layer: **Bring to Front**, **Bring Forward**, **Send Backward**, or **Send to Back**.

■ The layer assumes its new position in the stack.

Note: You cannot move a layer in back of the default Background layer.

CHANGE THE OPACITY OF A LAYER

Adjusting the opacity of a layer can let elements in the layers below show through. *Opacity* is the opposite of transparency. Decreasing the opacity of a layer increases its transparency.

CHANGE THE OPACITY OF A LAYER

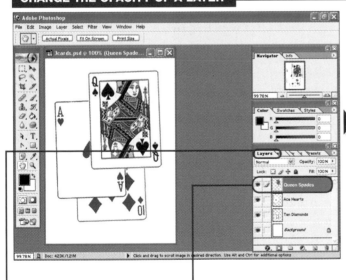

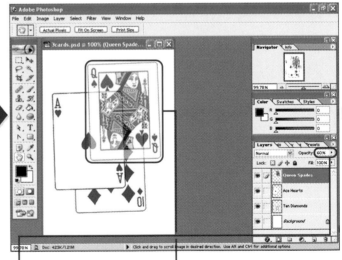

1 Click the **Layers** tab to select the Layers palette.

■ If the Layers tab is hidden, you can click **Window** and then **Layers** to open the Layers palette.

2 Click a layer other than the Background layer.

Note: You cannot change the opacity of the Background layer.

■ The default opacity is 100%, which is completely opaque.

3 Type a new value in the Opacity field.

■ Alternatively, you can click ► and drag the slider.

■ A layer's opacity can range from 0% to 100%.

■ The layer changes in opacity.

What is the Fill setting in the Layers palette?

It is similar to the Opacity setting, except that lowering it does not affect any blending options or layer styles applied to the layer. Lowering the Opacity *will* affect these settings. For more about blending options, see "Blend Layers." For more about layer styles, see Chapter 10.

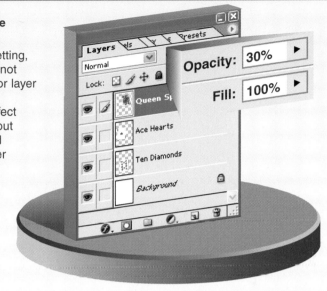

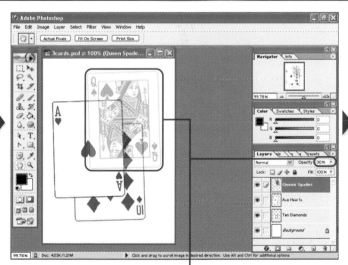

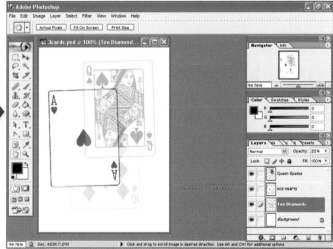

■ A shortcut for changing layer opacity is to click the layer and type a number key.

■ In this example, **3** was typed, which changes the opacity to 30%.

■ You can make multiple layers in your image semitransparent by changing their opacities.

■ In this example, both the Queen Spades and Ten Diamonds layers are semitransparent.

MERGE AND FLATTEN LAYERS

Merging layers lets you permanently combine information from two or more separate layers. Flattening layers combines all the layers of an image into one.

MERGE LAYERS

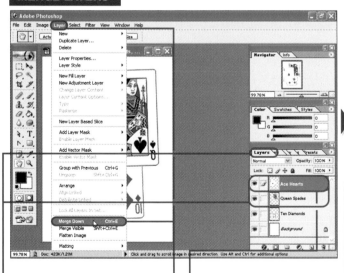

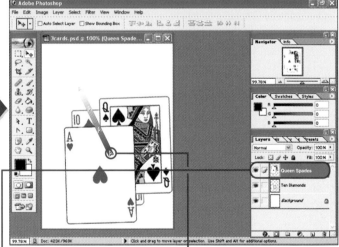

1 Click the **Layers** tab to select the Layers palette.

2 Place the two layers you want to merge next to each other.

Note: See the section "Reorder Layers" to change stacking order.

3 Click the topmost of the two layers.

4 Click **Layer**.

5 Click **Merge Down**.

■ The two layers merge.

■ Photoshop keeps the name of the lower layer.

■ To see the result of the merge, select the new layer, click ⊞, and click and drag the merged layer. The elements that were previously in separate layers now move together.

Why would I want to merge layers?

Merging layers enables you to save computer memory. The fewer layers a Photoshop image has, the less space it takes up in RAM and on your hard drive when you save it. Merging layers also lets you permanently combine elements of your image when you are happy with how you have arranged them relative to one another. If you want the option of rearranging all the original layers in the future, save a copy of your image before you merge layers.

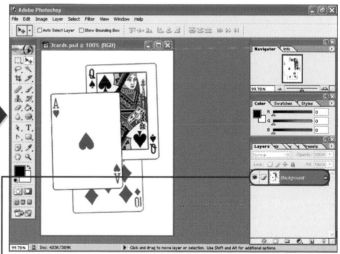

FLATTEN LAYERS

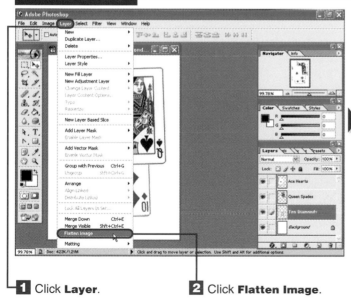

1 Click **Layer**.

2 Click **Flatten Image**.

■ All the layers merge into one.

RENAME A LAYER

You can rename a
layer to give it a
name that describes
its content.

RENAME A LAYER

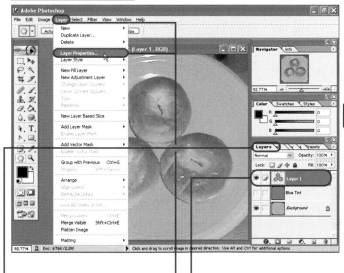

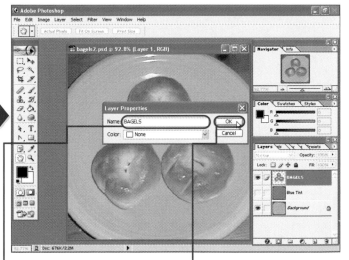

1 Click the **Layers** tab to
select the Layers palette.

■ If the Layers tab is hidden,
you can click **Window** and
then **Layers** to open the
Layers palette.

2 Click a layer.

3 Click **Layer**.

4 Click **Layer Properties**.

■ The Layer Properties
dialog box appears.

5 Type a new name for the
layer.

6 Click **OK**.

■ The name of the layer
changes in the Layers
palette.

You can use a transform
tool to change the shape
of the objects in a layer.
Transforming a layer
allows you to keep the
rest of your image
unchanged.

TRANSFORM A LAYER

1 Click the **Layers** tab to
select the Layers palette.

■ If the Layers tab is hidden,
you can click **Window** and
then **Layers** to open the
Layers palette.

2 Click **Edit**.

3 Click **Transform**.

4 Click a transform
command.

5 Click and drag the side
and corner handles to
transform the shape of the
layer.

6 Click ✓ or press **Enter**
(**Return**) to commit the
change.

■ You can click Ⓝ or press
Esc (⌘ + .) to cancel the
change.

*Note: For more about transforming
your images, see Chapter 5.*

CREATE A SOLID FILL LAYER

You can create a solid fill layer to place an opaque layer of color throughout your image.

CREATE A SOLID FILL LAYER

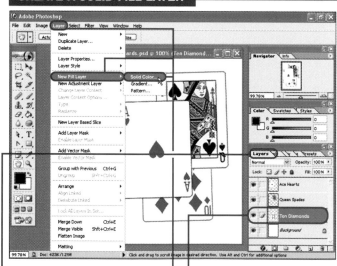

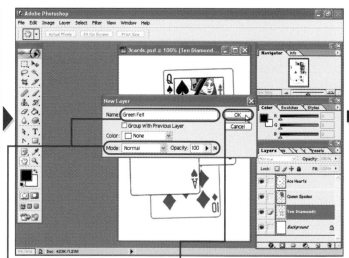

1 Click the **Layers** tab to select the Layers palette.

■ If the Layers tab is hidden, you can click **Window** and then **Layers** to open the Layers palette.

2 Click the layer above which you want to add solid color.

3 Click **Layer**.

4 Click **New Fill Layer**.

5 Click **Solid Color**.

■ The New Layer dialog box appears.

6 Type a name for the layer.

■ You can specify a type of blend mode or opacity setting for the layer.

Note: See "Blend Layers" or "Change the Opacity of a Layer" for details.

7 Click **OK**.

How do I add solid color to just part of a layer?

Make a selection with a selection tool before creating the solid fill layer. Photoshop adds color only inside the selection.

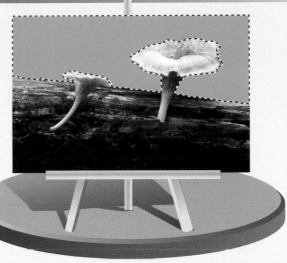

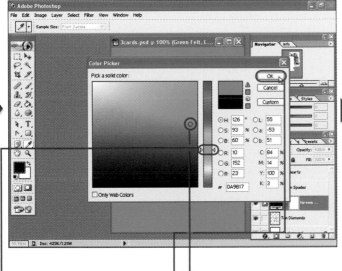

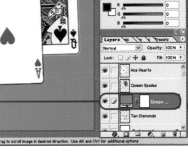

■ The Color Picker dialog box appears.

8 To change the range of colors that appears in the window, click and drag the slider (▷).

9 To select a fill color, click in the color window.

10 Click **OK**.

■ Photoshop creates a new layer filled with a solid color.

■ Layers above the new layer are not affected.

CREATE A GRADIENT FILL LAYER

You can create a
gradient fill layer to
place color transition
throughout your image.

For another way to add a
gradient to your image,
see Chapter 7.

CREATE A GRADIENT FILL LAYER

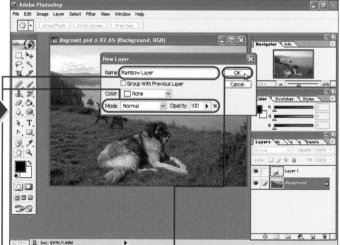

1 Click the **Layers** tab to
select the Layers palette.

■ If the Layers tab is hidden,
you can click **Window** and
then **Layers** to open the
Layers palette.

2 Click the layer above
which you want to add a
pattern.

3 Click **Layer**.

4 Click **New Fill Layer**.

5 Click **Gradient**.

■ The New Layer dialog box
appears.

6 Type a name for the layer.

■ You can specify a type of
blend or opacity setting for
the layer.

*Note: See the section "Blend Layers"
or "Change the Opacity of a Layer"
for details.*

7 Click **OK**.

Can I convert one type of fill layer to another?

Yes. Select the layer in the Layers palette. Click **Layer**, **Change Layer Content**, and then a different layer type.

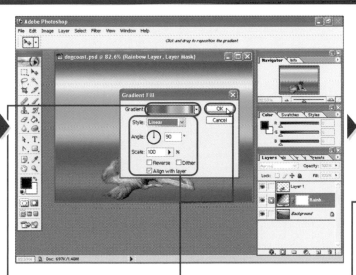

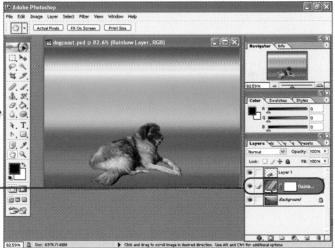

■ The Gradient Fill dialog box appears.

8 Click ⬍ (⬍).

9 Click a set of gradient colors from the menu that appears.

10 Select your other gradient settings.

■ You can select a style to specify the shape.

■ You can select an angle to specify the direction.

11 Click **OK**.

■ Photoshop creates a new layer filled with the specified gradient.

■ Layers above the new layer remain unaffected.

CREATE A PATTERN FILL LAYER

You can create a pattern fill layer to place repeating design throughout your image.

CREATE A PATTERN FILL LAYER

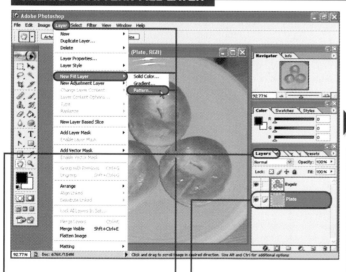

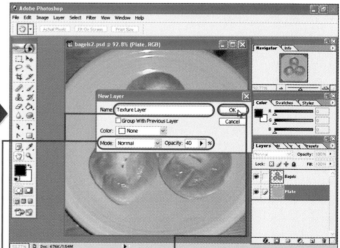

1 Click the **Layers** tab to select the Layers palette.

■ If the Layers tab is hidden, you can click **Window** and then **Layers** to open the Layers palette.

2 Click the layer above which you want to add a pattern.

3 Click **Layer**.

4 Click **New Fill Layer**.

5 Click **Pattern**.

■ The New Layer dialog box appears.

6 Type a name for the layer.

■ You can specify a type of blend mode or opacity setting for the layer.

■ In this example, the opacity is lowered so the plate layer shows through.

Note: See "Blend Layers" or "Change the Opacity of a Layer" for more details.

7 Click **OK**.

**How do I change the applied
pattern after creating the layer?**

Double-click the layer thumbnail in
the Layers palette. The Pattern Fill
dialog box appears and enables
you to edit the pattern.

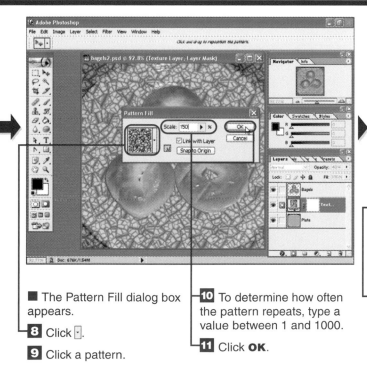

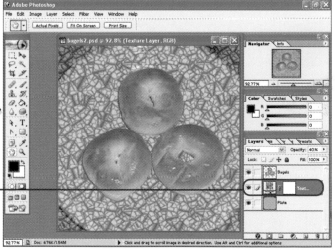

■ The Pattern Fill dialog box
appears.

8 Click ⬝.

9 Click a pattern.

10 To determine how often
the pattern repeats, type a
value between 1 and 1000.

11 Click **OK**.

■ Photoshop creates a new
layer filled with a pattern.

■ Layers above the new
layer remain unaffected.

CREATE AN ADJUSTMENT LAYER

Adjustment layers let you store color and tonal changes in a layer rather than having them permanently applied to your image.

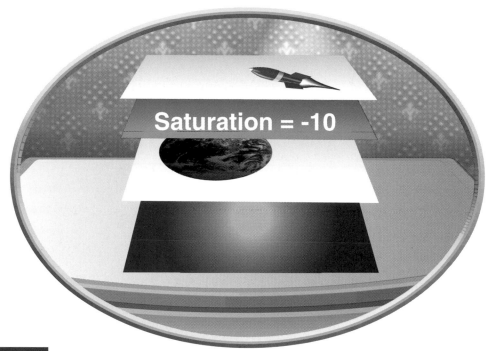

CREATE AN ADJUSTMENT LAYER

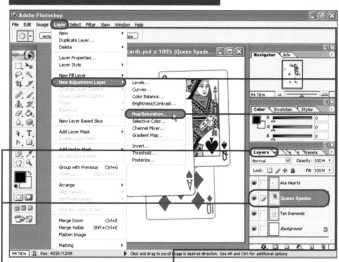

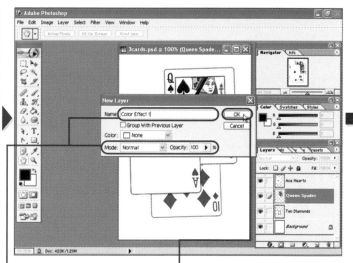

1 Click the **Layers** tab to select the Layers palette.

■ If the Layers tab is hidden, you can click **Window** and then **Layers** to open the Layers palette.

2 Click a layer.

3 Click **Layer**.

4 Click **New Adjustment Layer**.

5 Click an adjustment command.

■ The New Layer dialog box appears.

6 Type a name for the adjustment layer.

■ You can specify a type of blend or opacity setting for the layer.

Note: See the section "Blend Layers" or "Change the Opacity of a Layer" for details.

7 Click **OK**.

■ Photoshop places the new adjustment layer above the currently selected layer.

176

How do I apply an adjustment layer to only part of my image canvas?

Make a selection with a selection tool before creating the adjustment layer. See Chapter 4 for more on selection tools.

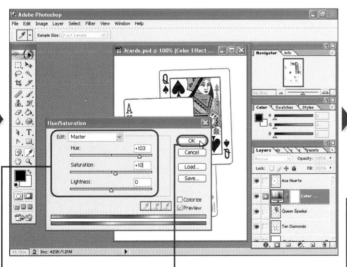

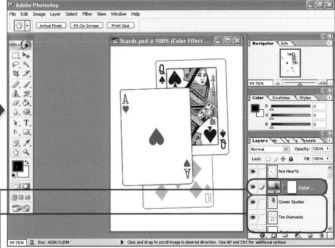

■ The dialog box for the adjustment command appears.

8 Click and drag the sliders (△) and type values to adjust the settings.

■ In this example, an adjustment layer is created that changes the hue and saturation.

9 Click **OK**.

■ Photoshop creates an adjustment layer.

■ Photoshop applies the effect to the layers below the adjustment layer.

■ In this example, Photoshop affects the card layers below the adjustment layer while leaving the card layer above it unaffected.

EDIT AN ADJUSTMENT LAYER

You can change the color and tonal changes that you defined in an adjustment layer. This lets you fine-tune your adjustment layer to get the effect you want.

EDIT AN ADJUSTMENT LAYER

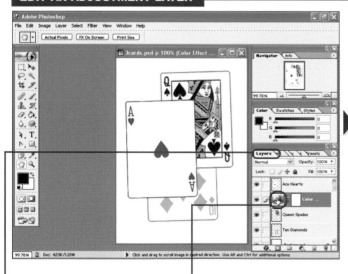

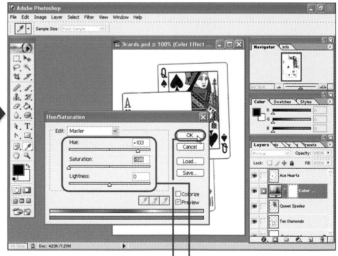

1 Click the **Layers** tab to select the Layers palette.

■ If the Layers tab is hidden, you can click **Window** and then **Layers** to open the Layers palette.

2 Double-click the adjustment layer icon (▣) in the Layers palette.

■ The settings dialog box corresponding to the adjustment command appears.

3 Click and drag the sliders (△) to change the settings in the dialog box.

4 Click **OK**.

How do I merge an adjustment layer with a regular layer?

Place the adjustment layer over the layer with which you want to merge it and then click **Layer** and **Merge Down**. When you merge the layers, Photoshop applies the adjustment layer's effects only to the layer with which you merged. The other layers below it remain unaffected.

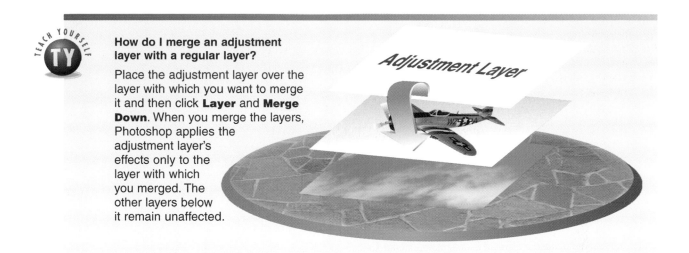

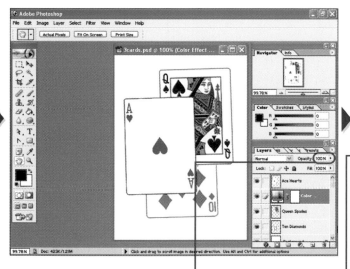

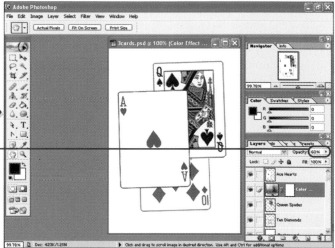

■ Photoshop applies your changes.

■ In this example, the saturation was reduced to the minimum, which removed the color in the layers below the adjustment layer.

■ You can lessen the effect of an adjustment layer by decreasing the layer's opacity to less than 100%.

■ In this example, the opacity was decreased to 60%, which reverses the decrease in saturation. Some of the original color in the cards returns.

LINK LAYERS

Linking causes different layers to move in unison when you move them with the Move tool. You may find linking useful when you want to keep elements of an image aligned with one another but do not want to merge their layers. See the section "Merge and Flatten Layers" for more on merging. Keeping layers unmerged lets you apply effects independently to each.

LINK LAYERS

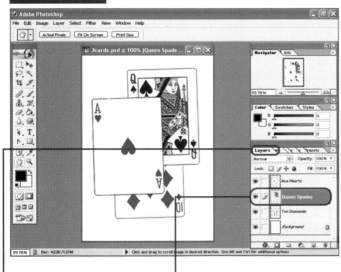

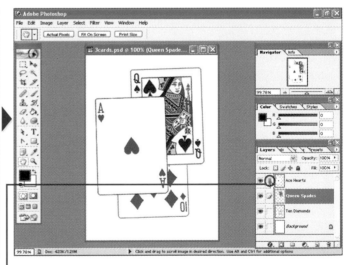

CREATE A LINK

1 Click the **Layers** tab to select the Layers palette.

■ If the Layers tab is hidden, you can click **Window** and then **Layers** to open the Layers palette.

2 Click one of the layers you want to link.

3 Click the box next to the other layer that you want to link.

■ Doing so turns on a linking icon (⬛).

■ The layers link together.

How do I keep from changing a layer after I have it the way I want it?

You can lock the layer by selecting the layer and clicking the Lock icon (🔒) located on the Layers palette (the button depresses and becomes highlighted). You cannot move, delete, or otherwise edit a locked layer. You can click the box to the left of the Transparency icon (🔲) if you just want to prevent a user from editing the transparent pixels in the layer.

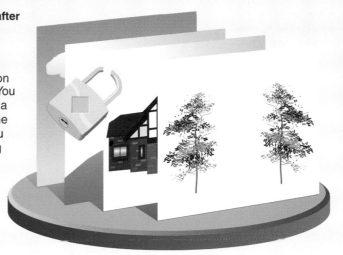

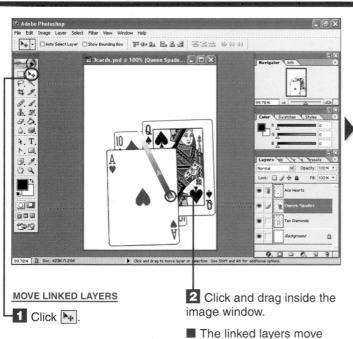

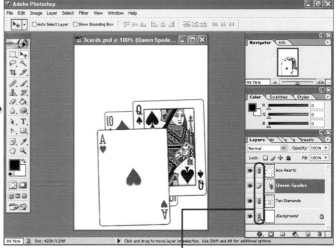

MOVE LINKED LAYERS

1 Click ✥.

2 Click and drag inside the image window.

■ The linked layers move together.

■ You can link as many layers as you like.

■ In this example, all the layers have been linked, including the Background layer.

BLEND LAYERS

You can use Photoshop's blending modes to specify how pixels in a layer blend with the layers below it.

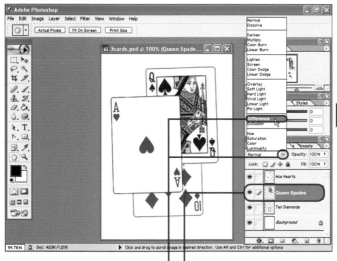

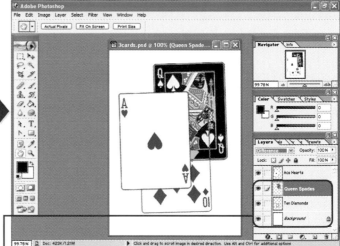

BLEND A REGULAR LAYER

1 Click the **Layers** tab to select the Layers palette.

■ If the Layers tab is hidden, you can click **Window** and then **Layers** to open the Layers palette.

2 Click the layer that you want to blend.

3 Click ☑ (⬍).

4 Click a blend mode.

■ Photoshop blends the selected layer with the layers below it.

■ This example shows the Difference mode, which creates a photo-negative effect where the selected layer overlaps other layers.

What effects do some of the different blending modes have?

The Multiply mode darkens the colors where the selected layer overlaps layers below it. The Screen mode is the opposite of Multiply; it lightens colors where layers overlap. Color takes the selected layer's colors and blends them with the details in the layers below it. Luminosity is the opposite of Color; it takes the selected layer's details and mixes them with the colors below it.

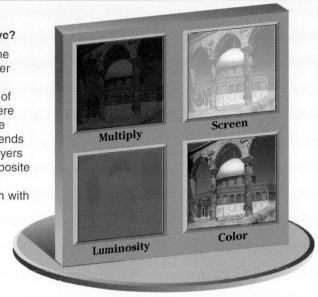

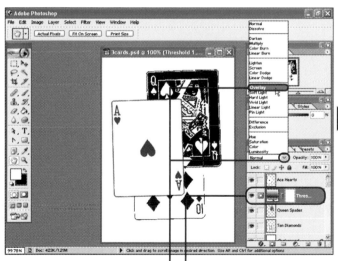

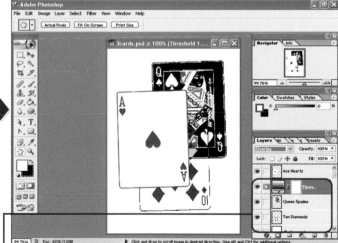

BLEND AN ADJUSTMENT LAYER

1 Click the **Layers** tab to select the Layers palette.

■ If the Layers tab is hidden, you can click **Window** and then **Layers** to open the Layers palette.

2 Click an adjustment layer that you want to blend.

3 Click ☑ (⬍).

4 Click a blend mode.

■ Photoshop blends the selected layer with the layers below it.

■ This example shows the Overlay mode applied to a Threshold adjustment layer, which lets some of the original color through.

EDIT LAYER EFFECT

APPLY OUTER GLOW?

...APPLYING DROP SHADOW...

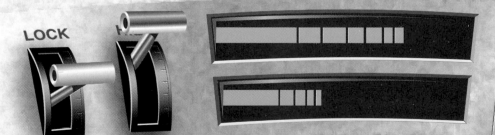

TY ANGLE LOCK DISTAN

CHAPTER 10

Applying Layer Effects

You can apply special effects to layers by applying Photoshop's built-in layer effects. The effects let you add shadows, glows, and 3D appearances to your layers. Photoshop's Styles palette lets you easily apply predefined combinations of effects to your image.

APPLY A DROP SHADOW

You can apply a drop shadow to make a layer look like it is raised off the image canvas.

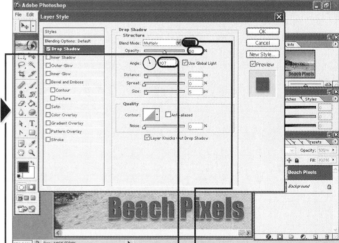

1 Click the **Layers** tab to select the Layers palette.

2 Click the layer to which you want to add the effect.

3 Click **Layer**.

4 Click **Layer Style**.

5 Click **Drop Shadow**.

■ You can also click the Layer Effects button ( ) and select **Drop Shadow**.

Note: Perform steps 6 through 11 if you want to enter your own settings. If you want to use the default settings, you can skip to step 12.

6 Type an Opacity value to specify the shadow's transparency.

7 Click the color swatch to select a shadow color.

Note: The default shadow color is black.

8 Type an Angle value to specify in which direction the shadow is displaced.

How do I add an inner shadow to a layer?

Click a layer and click **Layer**, **Layer Style**, and then **Inner Shadow**. An inner shadow creates a "cut out" effect, with the selected layer appearing to drop behind the image canvas.

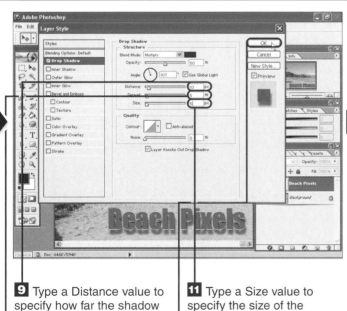

9 Type a Distance value to specify how far the shadow is displaced.

10 Type a Spread value to specify the fuzziness of the shadow's edge.

11 Type a Size value to specify the size of the shadow edge.

12 Click **OK**.

■ Photoshop creates a shadow in back of the selected layer.

■ The effect appears below the selected layer in the Layers palette.

Note: In this example, the effect was applied to a layer of type. For more information about type, see Chapter 13.

APPLY AN OUTER GLOW

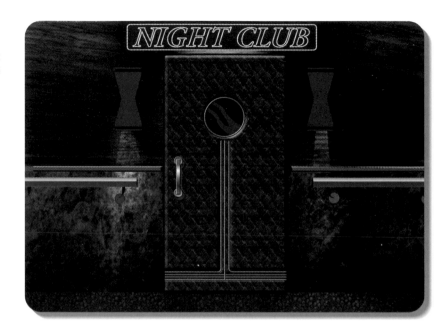

The outer glow effect adds faint coloring to the outside edge of a layer.

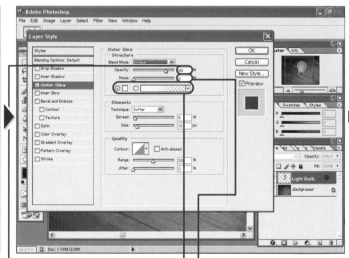

1 Click the **Layers** tab to select the Layers palette.

2 Click the layer to which you want to add the effect.

3 Click **Layer**.

4 Click **Layer Style**.

5 Click **Outer Glow**.

■ You can also click 🖉 and select **Outer Glow**.

*Note: Perform steps **6** through **10** if you want to enter your own Outer Glow settings. If you want to use the default settings, you can skip to step **11**.*

6 Type an Opacity value to specify the glow's darkness.

7 Specify a Noise value to add speckling to the glow.

8 Click the color swatch to choose the color of the glow (○ changes to ⊙). Or, you can choose from a series of preset color combinations by clicking ▾ .

How do I give elements in a layer an inner glow?

Click a layer and click **Layer**, **Layer Style**, and then **Inner Glow**. An inner glow adds color to the inside edge of a layer.

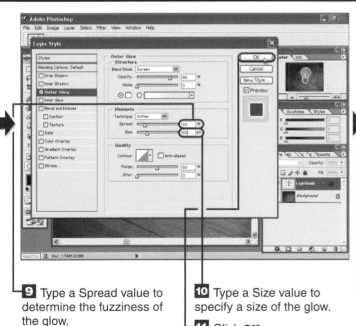

9 Type a Spread value to determine the fuzziness of the glow.

10 Type a Size value to specify a size of the glow.

11 Click **OK**.

■ Photoshop creates a glow around the outer edge of the selected layer.

APPLY BEVELING AND EMBOSSING

You can bevel and emboss a layer to give it a three-dimensional look.

APPLY BEVELING AND EMBOSSING

1 Click the **Layers** tab to select the Layers palette.

2 Click the layer to which you want to add the effect.

3 Click **Layer**.

4 Click **Layer Style**.

5 Click **Bevel and Emboss**.

■ You can also click and select **Bevel and Emboss**.

Note: Perform steps 6 through 9 if you want to enter your own settings. If you want to use the default settings, you can skip to step 10.

6 Select an effect style. Clicking **Inner Bevel** creates a three-dimensional look.

7 Specify the direction of the effect's shadowing (○ changes to ◉).

8 Type Depth and Size values to control the magnitude of the effect.

When would I use the Bevel and Emboss effect?

The effect can be useful for creating three-dimensional buttons for Web pages or multimedia applications. For example, to create such a 3D button, you can apply Bevel and Emboss to a colored rectangle and then lay type over it.

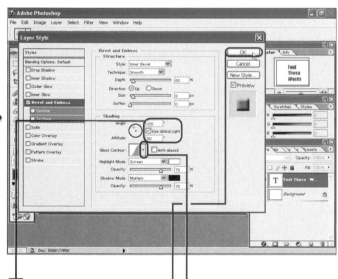

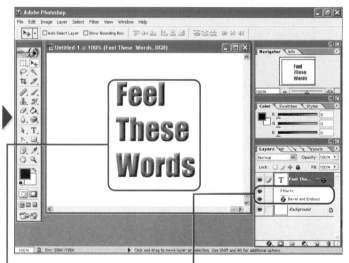

9 Specify the direction of the shading with the Angle and Altitude values.

■ You can click ⦁ and select one of the Gloss Contour settings to apply abstract effects to your layer.

10 Click **OK**.

■ Photoshop applies the bevel and emboss settings to the layer.

■ The effect appears below the selected layer in the Layers palette.

Note: In this example, the effect was applied to a layer of type. For more about type, see Chapter 13.

APPLY MULTIPLE EFFECTS TO A LAYER

You can apply multiple layer effects to layers in your image. This enables you to style your layers in complex ways.

APPLY MULTIPLE EFFECTS TO A LAYER

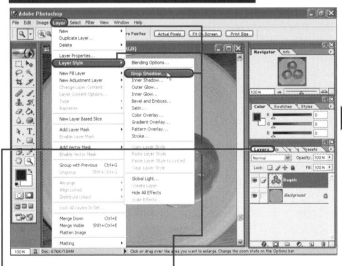

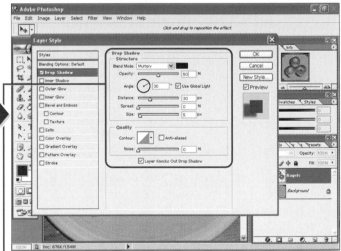

1 Click the **Layers** tab.

■ If the Layers tab is hidden, you can click **Window** and then **Layers**.

■ In this example, Drop Shadow and Color Overlay effects are applied.

2 Click **Layer**.

3 Click **Layer Style**.

4 Click the name of the first effect that you want to apply.

5 Specify the configuration values for the first effect.

How do I turn off layer effects that I have applied?

When you apply an effect to a layer, the effect gets added to the Layers palette. You may have to click ▶ to see a layer's effects (▶ changes to ▼). You can temporarily turn off an effect by clicking 👁 in the Layers palette. You can turn the effect on by clicking the now-empty box again to make 👁 reappear.

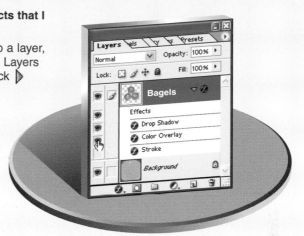

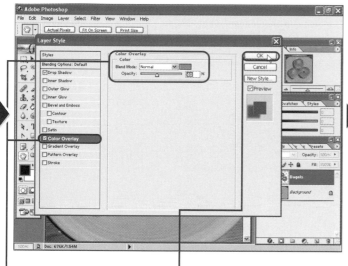

APPLY THE SECOND EFFECT

6 Click the next effect you want to apply (☐ changes to ☑).

7 Specify the configuration values for this effect.

■ In this example, a semitransparent green overlay is applied to the layer.

■ You can apply other effects to the layer by repeating steps **6** and **7**.

8 Click **OK**.

■ Photoshop applies the effects to the layer.

■ The effects appear below the selected layer in the Layers palette.

EDIT A LAYER EFFECT

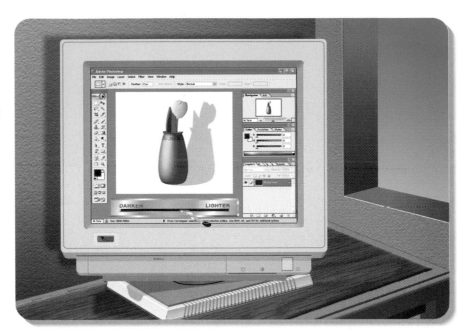

You can edit a layer effect that you have applied to your image. This lets you fine-tune the effect to achieve an appearance that suits you.

EDIT A LAYER EFFECT

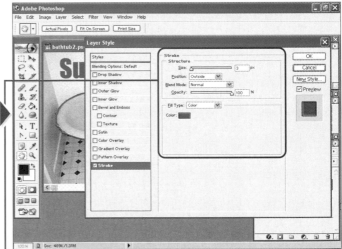

1 Click the **Layers** tab.

■ If the Layers tab is hidden, you can click **Window** and then **Layers**.

■ This example shows editing the color stroked around a layer object.

2 Click **Layer**.

3 Click **Layer Style**.

4 Click the effect you want to edit.

■ You can also double-click the effect in the Layers palette.

■ Photoshop displays the current configuration values for the effect.

How do I keep a layer effect from accidentally being changed?

You can lock a layer and its effects by selecting the layer and checking the 🔒 in the Layers palette (the button depresses and becomes highlighted). The layer is then locked, which means that you cannot change its styles or apply any more Photoshop commands to it. You can also click ▣, ✎, or ⊹ to lock a layer's transparent pixels, all of its pixels, or its position, respectively.

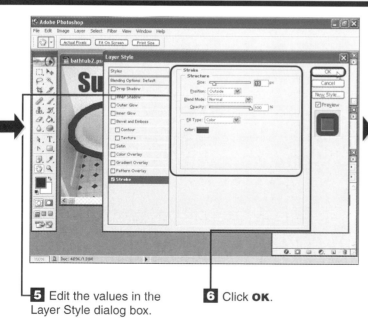

5 Edit the values in the Layer Style dialog box.

■ This example shows broadening and recoloring of the stroke effect.

6 Click **OK**.

■ Photoshop applies the edited effect to the layer.

■ You can edit an effect as many times as you want.

APPLY STYLES

You can apply a Photoshop style to a layer to give the layer a colorful or textured look. Styles are predefined combinations of Photoshop effects that are stored in the Styles palette.

APPLY STYLES

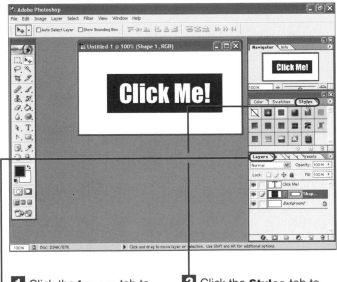

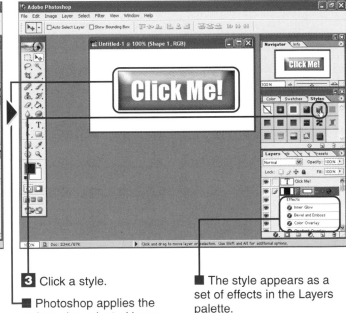

1 Click the **Layers** tab to select the Layers palette.

■ If the Layers tab is hidden, you can click **Window** and then **Layers** to open the Layers palette.

2 Click the **Styles** tab to display Photoshop's styles.

■ If the Styles tab is hidden, you can click **Window** and then **Styles** to open the Styles palette.

3 Click a style.

■ Photoshop applies the style to the selected layer.

■ The style appears as a set of effects in the Layers palette.

How do I create my own custom styles?

To create a custom style, first apply one or more effects — such as Drop Shadow, Outer Glow, and others — to a layer in your image. With the layer selected in the Layers palette, click the Styles ⊙ and click **New Style**. A dialog box appears that lets you name your custom style. Click **OK** in the dialog box to add an icon for your new style to the Styles palette.

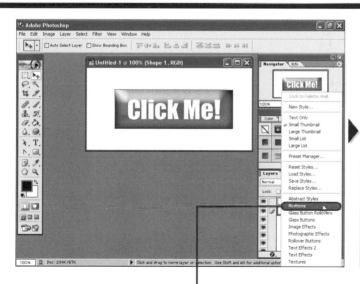

ACCESS MORE STYLES

1 Click the Styles ⊙.

2 Click a set of styles.

■ Photoshop displays a dialog box that lets you replace the current styles with the new set or append the new set.

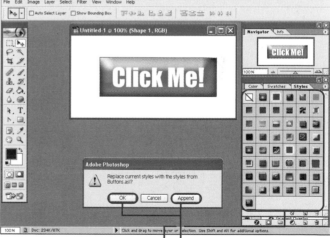

3 Click **OK** or **Append**.

■ Photoshop adds the new styles to the Styles palette.

■ In this example, the new styles have been appended to the current ones.

CHAPTER 11

Applying Filters

With Photoshop's filters, you can quickly and easily apply enhancements to your image, including artistic effects, texture effects, and distortions. Filters can help you correct defects in your images or let you turn a photograph into something resembling an impressionist painting. Photoshop comes with more than 100 filters; this chapter highlights only a few. For details about all the filters, see the Help documentation.

TURN AN IMAGE INTO A PAINTING

You can use many of Photoshop's artistic filters to make your image look as though it was created with a paintbrush. The Dry Brush filter, for example, applies a painted effect by converting similarly colored areas in your image to solid colors.

TURN AN IMAGE INTO A PAINTING

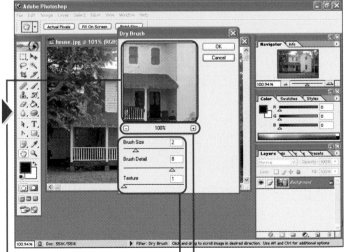

1 Select the layer to which you want to apply the filter.

■ To apply the filter to just part of your image, make a selection with a selection tool.

Note: For more about layers, see Chapter 9. See Chapter 4 to use selection tools.

■ In this example, the image has a single background layer.

2 Click **Filter**.

3 Click **Artistic**.

4 Click **Dry Brush**.

■ The Dry Brush dialog box appears.

■ A small window displays a preview of the filter's effect.

■ Click ⊟ or ⊞ to zoom out or in.

5 Fine-tune the filter effect by typing values for the Brush Size, Brush Detail, and Texture.

What does the Sponge filter do?

The Sponge filter reduces detail and modifies the shapes in an image to create the effect you get when applying a damp sponge to a wet painting. Apply it by clicking **Filter**, **Artistic**, and then **Sponge**.

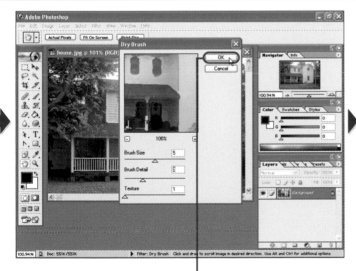

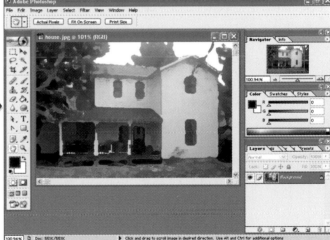

■ This example shows how to thicken the dry-brush effect by increasing Brush Size and decreasing Brush Detail.

6 Click **OK**.

■ Photoshop applies the filter.

BLUR AN IMAGE

Photoshop's Blur filters reduce the amount of detail in your image. The Gaussian Blur filter has advantages over the other Blur filters in that you can control the amount of blur added.

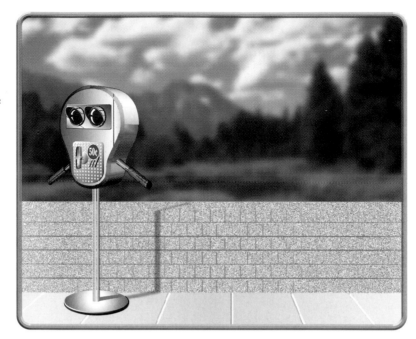

BLUR AN IMAGE

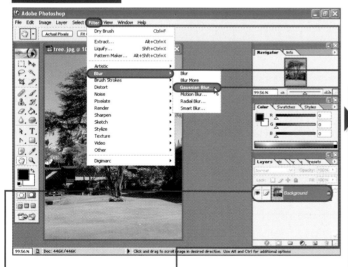

1 Select the layer to which you want to apply the filter.

■ To apply the filter to just part of your image, make a selection with a selection tool.

Note: For more about layers, see Chapter 9. To use the selection tools, see Chapter 4.

■ In this example, the image has a single background layer.

2 Click **Filter**.

3 Click **Blur**.

4 Click **Gaussian Blur**.

■ The Gaussian Blur dialog box appears.

■ A small window displays a preview of the filter's effect.

■ Click − or + to zoom out or in.

5 Click **Preview** to preview the effect in the main window (☐ changes to ☑).

6 Click and drag the Radius slider (△) to control the amount of blur added.

How do I add directional blurring to an image?

You can add directional blur to your image with the Motion Blur filter. This can add a sense of motion to your image. Apply it by selecting **Filter**, **Blur**, and then **Motion Blur**.

APPLY MOTION BLUR

■ In this example, the amount of blur has been increased by boosting the Radius value.

7 Click **OK**.

■ Photoshop applies the filter.

SHARPEN AN IMAGE

Photoshop's Sharpen filters intensify the detail and reduce blurring in your image. The Unsharp Mask filter has advantages over the other Sharpen filters in that it lets you control the amount of sharpening you apply.

SHARPEN AN IMAGE

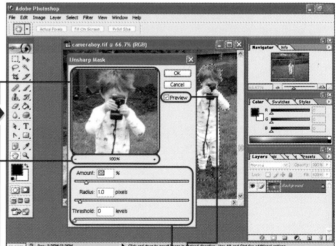

■ **1** Select the layer to which you want to apply the filter.

■ To apply the filter to just part of your image, make a selection with a selection tool.

Note: For more about layers, see Chapter 9. To use the selection tools, see Chapter 4.

■ In this example, the filter is applied to a selection.

2 Click **Filter**.

3 Click **Sharpen**.

4 Click **Unsharp Mask**.

■ The Unsharp Mask dialog box appears.

■ A small window displays a preview of the filter's effect.

■ Click − or + to zoom out or in.

5 Click **Preview** to preview the effect in the main window (☐ changes to ☑).

6 Click and drag the sliders (△) to control the amount of sharpening you apply to the image.

**When should I apply
sharpening?**

It is a good idea to
sharpen an image
after you have
changed its size
because changing an
image's size will add
blurring. Applying the
Unsharp Mask filter
can also help clarify
scanned images.

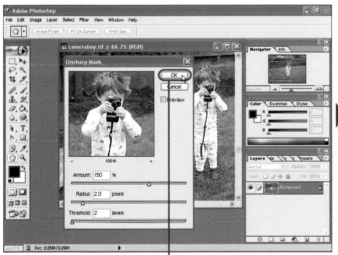

■ **Amount** controls the
overall amount of sharpening.

■ **Radius** controls whether
sharpening is confined to
edges in the image (low
Radius setting) or added
across the entire image
(high Radius setting).

■ **Threshold** controls how
much contrast you must
have present for an edge
to be recognized and
sharpened.

7 Click **OK**.

■ Photoshop applies the
filter.

DISTORT AN IMAGE

Photoshop's Distort filters stretch and squeeze areas of your image. For example, the Spherize filter produces a fun-house effect. It makes your image look like it is being reflected off a mirrored sphere.

You can also distort an image by using the Distort command, located under the Edit menu. See Chapter 5 for more information.

DISTORT AN IMAGE

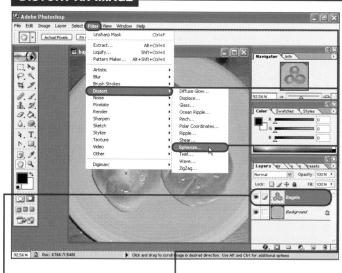

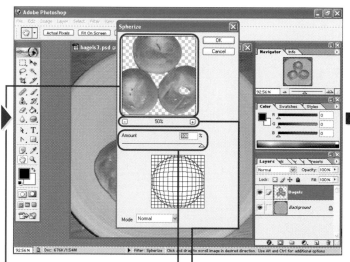

1 Select the layer to which you want to apply the filter.

■ To apply the filter to just part of your image, make a selection with a selection tool.

Note: For more about layers, see Chapter 9. See Chapter 4 to use the selection tools.

2 Click **Filter**.

3 Click **Distort**.

4 Click **Spherize**.

■ The Spherize dialog box appears.

■ A small window displays a preview of the filter's effect.

■ Click ▣ or ▣ to zoom out or in.

5 Click and drag the Amount slider (△) to control the amount of distortion added.

What happens when I type a negative value in the Amount field of the Spherize dialog box?

A negative value "squeezes" the shapes in your image instead of expanding them. The Pinch filter — which you can also find under the **Filter** and **Distort** menu selections — produces a similar effect.

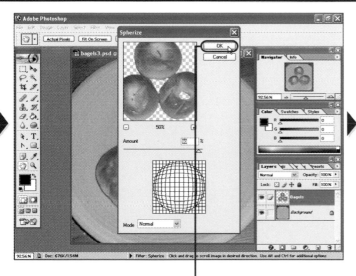

■ In this example, the intensity of the spherize effect has been decreased.

6 Click **OK**.

■ Photoshop applies the filter.

ADD NOISE TO AN IMAGE

Filters in the Noise menu add or remove graininess in your image. You can add graininess with the Add Noise filter.

ADD NOISE TO AN IMAGE

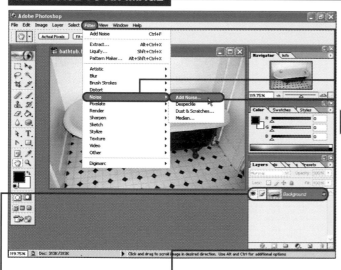

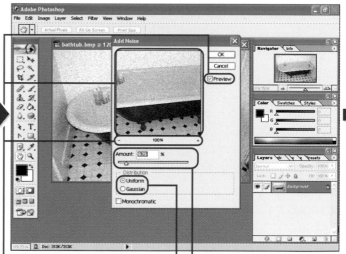

1 Select the layer to which you want to apply the filter.

■ To apply the filter to just part of your image, make a selection with a selection tool.

Note: For more about layers, see Chapter 9. To use the selection tools, see Chapter 4.

■ In this example, the image has a single background layer.

2 Click **Filter**.

3 Click **Noise**.

4 Click **Add Noise**.

■ The Add Noise dialog box appears.

■ A small window displays a preview.

■ Click ― or + to zoom out or in.

5 Click **Preview** to preview the effect in the main window (☐ changes to ☑).

6 Click and drag the Amount slider (△) to control the amount of noise added.

7 Select the way you want the noise distributed (○ changes to ◉).

■ Uniform spreads the noise more evenly than Gaussian.

What does the Monochromatic setting in the Add Noise dialog box do?

If you click **Monochromatic** (☐ changes to ☑), Photoshop adds noise by lightening or darkening pixels in your image. Pixel hues stay the same. At high settings with the Monochromatic setting on, the filter produces a television-static effect.

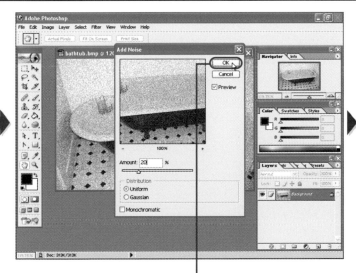

■ In this example, the Amount value has been increased.

8 Click **OK**.

■ Photoshop applies the filter.

TURN AN IMAGE INTO SHAPES

The Pixelate filters divide areas of your image into solid-colored dots or shapes. The Crystallize filter, one example of a Pixelate filter, re-creates your image using colored polygons.

TURN AN IMAGE INTO SHAPES

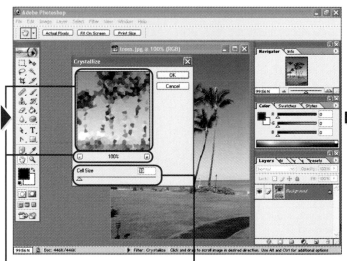

1 Select the layer to which you want to apply the filter.

■ To apply the filter to just part of your image, make a selection with a selection tool.

Note: For more about layers, see Chapter 9. To use the selection tools, see Chapter 4.

■ In this example, the image has a single background layer.

2 Click **Filter**.

3 Click **Pixelate**.

4 Click **Crystallize**.

■ The Crystallize dialog box appears.

■ A small window displays a preview of the filter's effect.

■ Click 🔲 or 🔳 to zoom out or in.

5 Click and drag the Cell Size slider (△) to adjust the size of the shapes.

■ The size can range from 3 to 300.

What does the Mosaic filter do?

The Mosaic filter converts your image to a set of solid-color squares. You can control the size of the squares in the filter's dialog box. Apply it by clicking **Filter**, **Pixelate**, and then **Mosaic**.

■ In this example, the Cell Size has been slightly increased.

6 Click **OK**.

■ Photoshop applies the filter.

TURN AN IMAGE INTO A CHARCOAL SKETCH

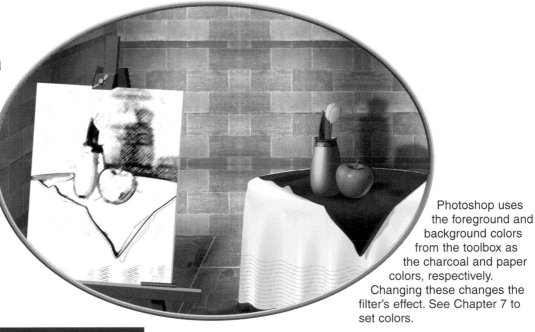

The Sketch filters add outlining effects to your image. The Charcoal filter, for example, makes an image look as if you have sketched it by using charcoal on paper.

Photoshop uses the foreground and background colors from the toolbox as the charcoal and paper colors, respectively. Changing these changes the filter's effect. See Chapter 7 to set colors.

TURN AN IMAGE INTO A CHARCOAL SKETCH

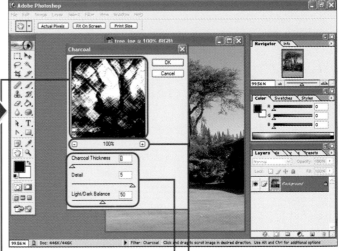

■1 Select the layer to which you want to apply the filter.

■ To apply the filter to just part of your image, make a selection with a selection tool.

Note: For more about layers, see Chapter 9. To use the selection tools, see Chapter 4.

■ In this example, the image has a single background layer.

■2 Click **Filter**.

■3 Click **Sketch**.

■4 Click **Charcoal**.

■ The Charcoal dialog box appears.

■ A small window displays a preview of the filter's effect.

■ Click 🔲 or 🔲 to zoom out or in.

■5 Click and drag the sliders (△) to control the filter's effect.

What does the Photocopy filter do?

The Photocopy filter converts shadows and midtones in your image to the foreground color in the toolbox and highlights in your image to the background color. The result is an image that looks photocopied. You can apply the Photocopy filter by clicking **Filter**, **Sketch**, and then **Photocopy**.

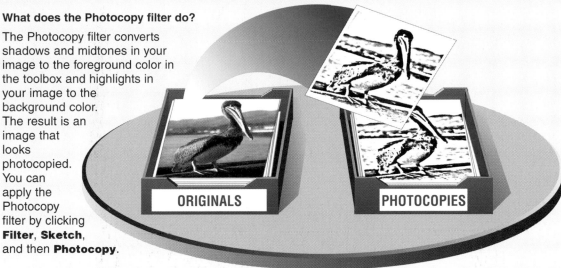

ORIGINALS

PHOTOCOPIES

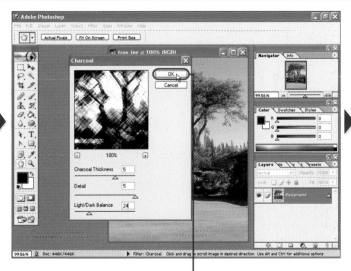

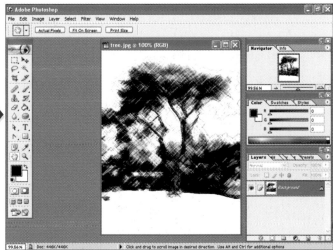

■ In this example, the thickness of the charcoal strokes has been increased. The Light/Dark Balance setting has also been decreased.

6 Click **OK**.

■ Photoshop applies the filter.

APPLY GLOWING EDGES TO AN IMAGE

The Glowing Edges filter, one example of a Stylize filter, applies a neon effect to the edges in your image. Areas between the edges turn black. Other Stylize filters produce similarly extreme artistic effects.

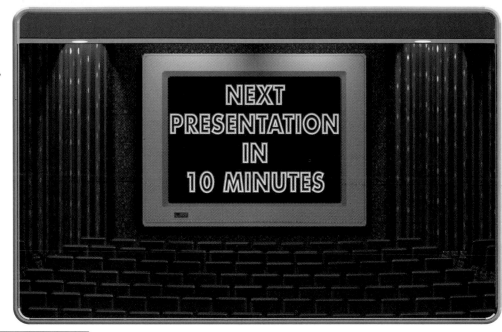

APPLY GLOWING EDGES TO AN IMAGE

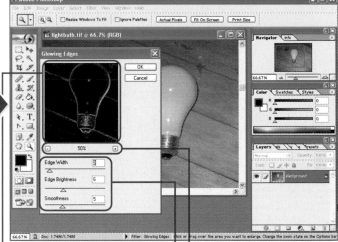

■ **1** Select the layer to which you want to apply the filter.

■ To apply the filter to just part of your image, make a selection with a selection tool.

Note: For more about layers, see Chapter 9. To use the selection tools, see Chapter 4.

■ In this example, the image has a single background layer.

2 Click **Filter**.

3 Click **Stylize**.

4 Click **Glowing Edges**.

■ The Glowing Edges dialog box appears.

■ A small window displays a preview of the filter's effect.

■ Click 🔲 or ⊞ to zoom out or in.

5 Click and drag the sliders (△) to control the intensity of the glow you add to the edges in the image.

How can I quickly add wild special effects to my images?

Many of the filters in the Stylize menu produce out-of-this-world effects. The Emboss and Solarize filters are two examples.

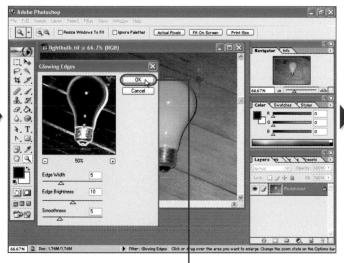

■ In this example, the Edge Width and Edge Brightness values have been increased to intensify the neon effect.

6 Click **OK**.

■ Photoshop applies the filter.

ADD TEXTURE TO AN IMAGE

You can overlay different textures on your image with the Texturizer filter. The other Texture filters let you apply other patterns.

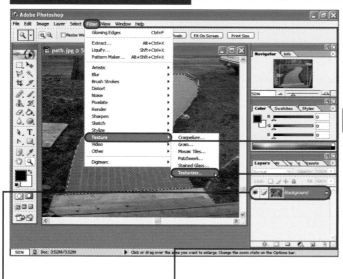

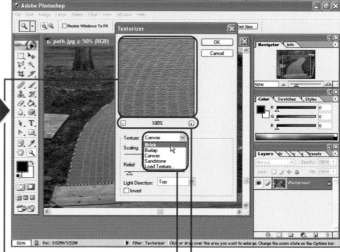

■1 Select the layer to which you want to apply the filter.

■ To apply the filter to just part of your image, make a selection with a selection tool.

Note: For more about layers, see Chapter 9. See Chapter 4 to use the selection tools.

■ In this example, the filter is applied to a selection.

■2 Click **Filter**.

■3 Click **Texture**.

■4 Click **Texturizer**.

■ The Texturizer dialog box appears.

■ A small window displays a preview of the filter's effect.

■ Click ⊟ or ⊞ to zoom out or in.

■5 Click ⊡ (⊡) and select a texture to apply.

216

What does the Stained Glass filter do?

The Stained Glass filter converts small areas of your image to different solid-color shapes, similar to those you might see in a stained-glass window. A foreground-color border separates the shapes. Apply it by selecting **Filter**, **Texture**, and then **Stained Glass**.

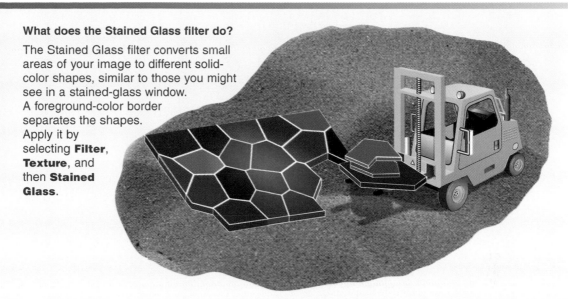

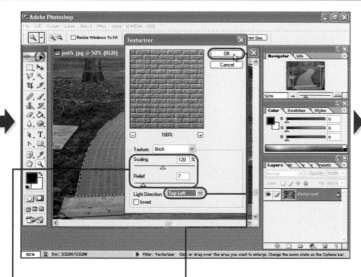

6 Click and drag the sliders (⌂) to control the intensity of the overlaid texture.

7 Click ▼ (⬍) and select a Light Direction.

8 Click **OK**.

■ Photoshop applies the filter.

217

OFFSET AN IMAGE

The filters in the Other submenu produce interesting effects that do not fall under the other menu descriptions. For example, you can shift your image horizontally or vertically in the image window using the Other menu's Offset filter.

OFFSET AN IMAGE

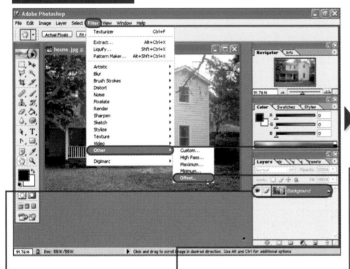

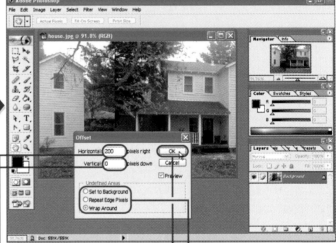

1 Select the layer to which you want to apply the filter.

■ If you want to apply the filter to just a select part of your image, make a selection with a selection tool.

Note: For more about layers, see Chapter 9. See Chapter 4 to use the selection tools.

■ In this example, the image has a single background layer.

2 Click **Filter**.

3 Click **Other**.

4 Click **Offset**.

■ The Offset dialog box appears.

5 Type a horizontal offset.

6 Type a vertical offset.

7 Select how you want Photoshop to treat pixels at the edge (○ changes to ◉).

8 Click **OK**.

How do I make a seamless tile?

Seamless tiles are images that when laid side by side leave no noticeable seam where they meet. You often use them as background images for Web pages. To create a seamless tile, start with an evenly textured image; then offset the image horizontally and vertically; then clean up the resulting seams with the Clone Stamp tool ([icon]). See Chapter 7 for information on using the Clone Stamp tool. The resulting image tiles seamlessly when you use it as a Web page background.

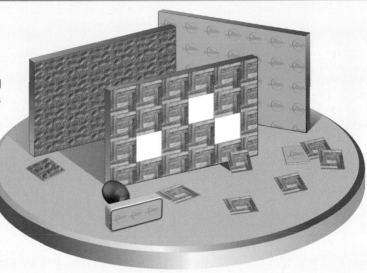

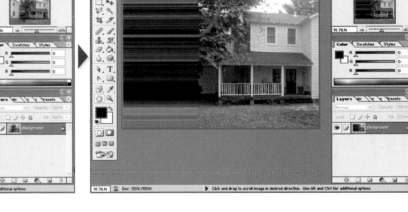

■ In this example, the image has been shifted horizontally (to the right) by adding a positive value to the horizontal field.

■ Wrap Around was selected, so the pixels cropped from the right edge of the image reappear on the left edge.

■ In this example, the same offset was applied but with Repeat Edge Pixels selected. This creates a streaked effect at the left edge.

USING THE LIQUIFY TOOLS

Photoshop's Liquify tools enable you to dramatically warp areas of your image. The tools are useful for making your image look like it is melting.

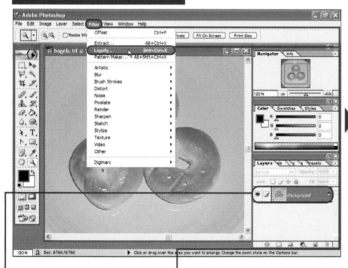

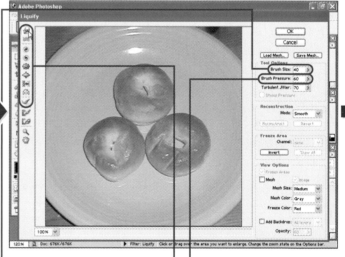

1 Select the layer to which you want to apply the Liquify tool.

■ To apply the filter to just a select part of your image, make a selection with a selection tool.

Note: For more about layers, see Chapter 9. See Chapter 4 to use the selection tools.

■ In this example, the image has a single background layer.

2 Click **Filter**.

3 Click **Liquify**.

■ The Liquify dialog box displays.

4 Type a Brush Size from 1 to 600.

5 Type a Brush Pressure (strength) from 1 to 100.

6 Click a Liquify tool.

■ The example makes use of the Warp tool.

What do the different Liquify tools do?

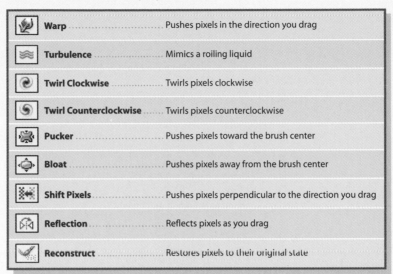

	Warp	Pushes pixels in the direction you drag
	Turbulence	Mimics a roiling liquid
	Twirl Clockwise	Twirls pixels clockwise
	Twirl Counterclockwise	Twirls pixels counterclockwise
	Pucker	Pushes pixels toward the brush center
	Bloat	Pushes pixels away from the brush center
	Shift Pixels	Pushes pixels perpendicular to the direction you drag
	Reflection	Reflects pixels as you drag
	Reconstruct	Restores pixels to their original state

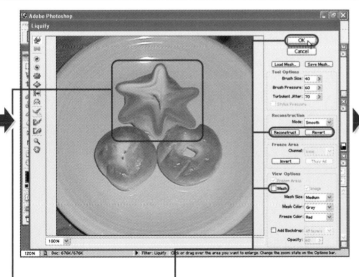

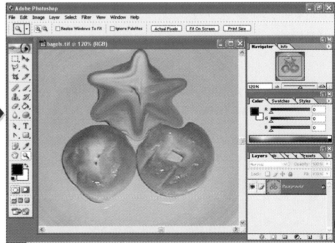

7 Click and drag inside the image window.

■ Photoshop liquifies the image where you drag the brush.

■ You can click **Reconstruct** or **Revert** to change the image back to its original state.

■ You can click **Mesh** (□ changes to ☑) to overlay a grid to measure your changes.

8 Click **OK**.

■ Photoshop applies the Liquify effect to your image.

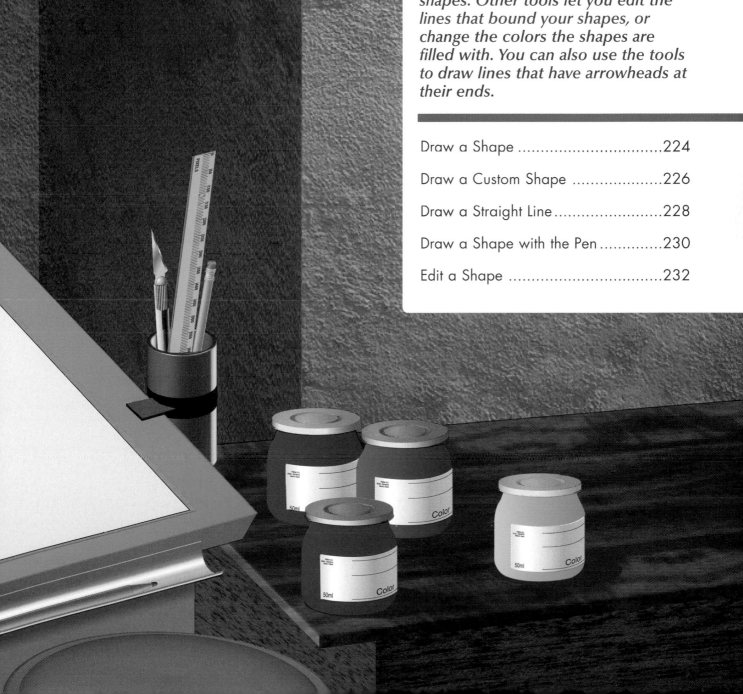

CHAPTER 12

Drawing Shapes

Photoshop offers a variety of tools for drawing geometric and abstract shapes. Other tools let you edit the lines that bound your shapes, or change the colors the shapes are filled with. You can also use the tools to draw lines that have arrowheads at their ends.

DRAW A SHAPE

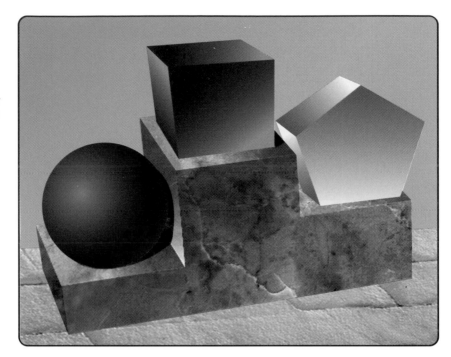

You can create solid shapes in your image using Photoshop's many shape tools. This makes it easy to create solid decorations for your photos or buttons for your Web site.

DRAW A SHAPE

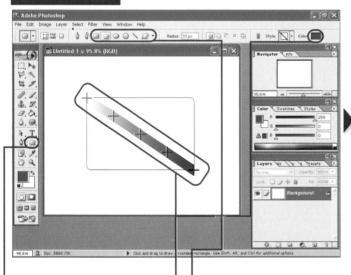

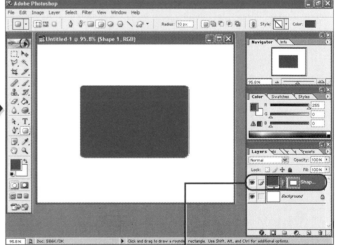

DRAW A SOLID SHAPE

1 Click the Shape tool (⬜).

Note: The tool icon may differ, depending on what type of shape you drew last.

2 Click a shape in the Options bar.

3 Click the Color box to select a color for the shape.

Note: For details on selecting colors, see Chapter 7.

4 Click and drag to draw the shape.

■ Photoshop draws the shape and fills it with the specified color.

■ The shape appears in a new layer in the Layers palette.

How do I resize a shape after I draw it?

Click the shape's layer and then click the Shape tool ([□]). Click **Image**, **Transform Shape**, and then a transform command. You can then resize the shape just like you would a selection. See Chapter 5 for details on transforming selections.

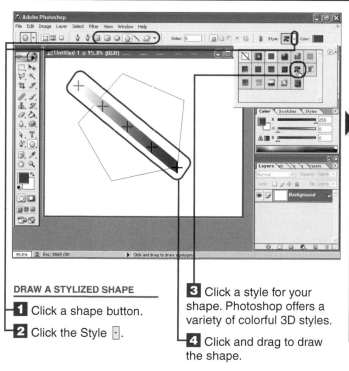

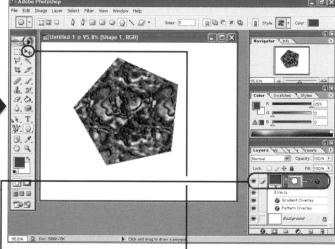

DRAW A STYLIZED SHAPE

1 Click a shape button.

2 Click the Style ⏷.

3 Click a style for your shape. Photoshop offers a variety of colorful 3D styles.

4 Click and drag to draw the shape.

■ Photoshop draws the shape and styles it with the specified style.

■ The shape appears in a new layer in the Layers palette.

Note: For more about layers, see Chapter 9.

■ You can move the shape by selecting its layer and using the Move tool ([▶₊]).

Note: For more about the Move tool, see Chapter 5.

DRAW A CUSTOM SHAPE

You can use the Custom Shape tool to draw a variety of interesting predefined shapes, including animals, frames, and talk bubbles.

DRAW A CUSTOM SHAPE

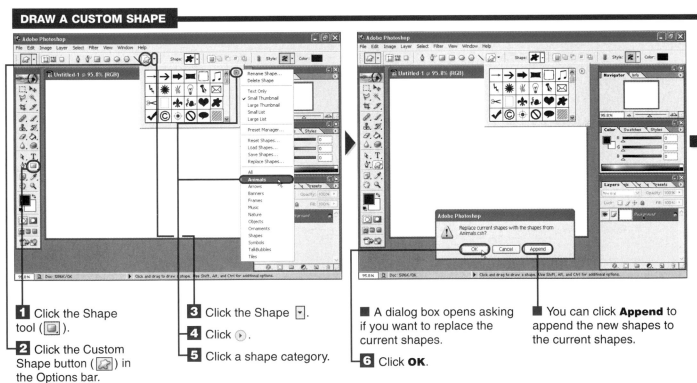

1 Click the Shape tool (▢).

2 Click the Custom Shape button (▨) in the Options bar.

3 Click the Shape ▾.

4 Click ⊙.

5 Click a shape category.

■ A dialog box opens asking if you want to replace the current shapes.

6 Click **OK**.

■ You can click **Append** to append the new shapes to the current shapes.

How do I overlap shapes in interesting ways?

To determine how overlapping shapes interact, click one of the following options in the Options bar before drawing:

Add to Shape Area () adds a shape area to another shape area.

Subtract from Shape Area () subtracts a shape area from another shape area.

Intersect Shape Areas () keeps the area where shapes intersect.

Exclude Overlapping Shape Areas () keeps the area where shapes do not overlap.

ADD TO SHAPE AREA	**SUBTRACT FROM SHAPE**
INTERSECT OVERLAPPING SHAPE AREAS	**EXCLUDE OVERLAPPING SHAPE AREAS**

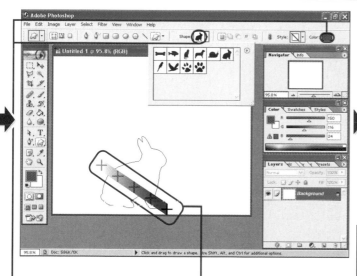

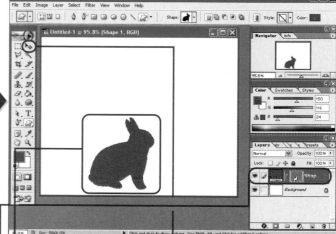

7 Click a shape.

8 Click the Color box to select a color for the shape.

Note: For details on selecting colors, see Chapter 7.

9 Click and drag to draw the shape.

■ Photoshop draws the shape and fills it with the specified color.

■ The shape appears in a new layer in the Layers palette.

Note: For more about layers, see Chapter 9.

■ You can move the shape by selecting its layer and using the Move tool ().

Note: For more about the Move tool, see Chapter 5.

DRAW A STRAIGHT LINE

You can draw a straight line using Photoshop's Shape tool. You can customize the line with arrows, giving you an easy way to point out elements in your image.

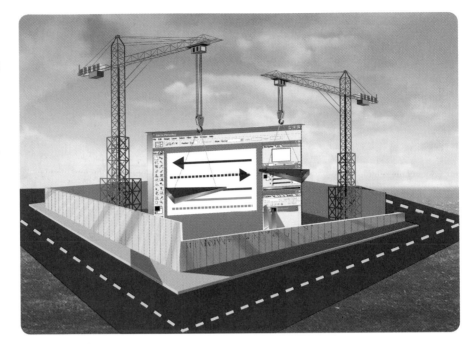

DRAW A STRAIGHT LINE

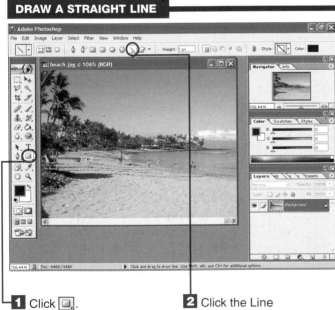

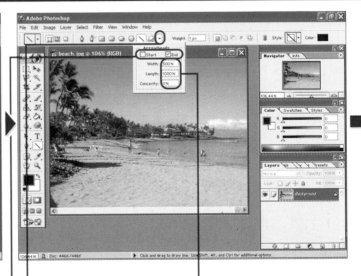

1 Click ▣.

Note: The tool icon may differ, depending on what type of shape you drew last.

2 Click the Line button (◯).

3 Click the tool ▾.

4 Click **Start** or **End** to include arrowheads on your line (☐ changes to ☑).

■ You can also specify the shape of the arrowheads by typing values here.

5 Press Enter (Return) to close the menu.

**How do I draw a horizontal or
vertical line?**

Press **Shift** as you click and drag
to create your line. You can also
use this technique to drag lines at
45-degree diagonals.

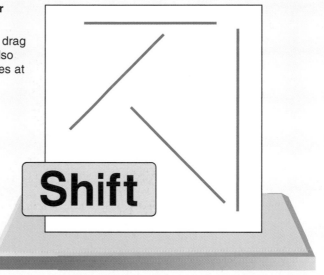

6 Type a line weight.

7 Click the Layer Style ⏷.

8 Click a style for your line.

■ The Default Style (⬚)
creates a plain, solid line.

9 Press **Enter** (**Return**) to
close the menu.

■ You can click the Color
box to select a different line
color.

10 Click and drag to draw
the line.

■ Photoshop places the line
in its own layer.

Note: For more about layers, see
Chapter 9.

■ You can move the shape
by selecting its layer and
using the Move tool (▶⊕).

Note: For more about the Move tool,
see Chapter 5.

DRAW A SHAPE WITH THE PEN

The Pen tool lets you create shapes by drawing the lines yourself. This allows you to make shapes that are not in Photoshop's predefined menus.

DRAW A SHAPE WITH THE PEN

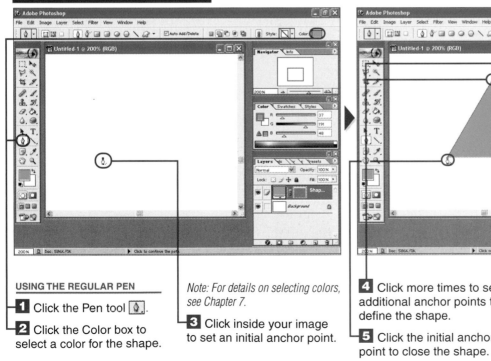

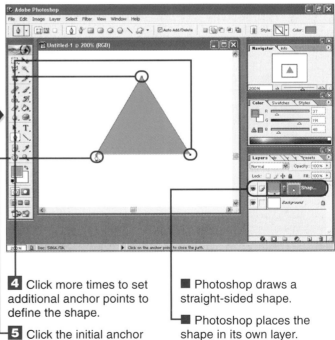

USING THE REGULAR PEN

1 Click the Pen tool.

2 Click the Color box to select a color for the shape.

Note: For details on selecting colors, see Chapter 7.

3 Click inside your image to set an initial anchor point.

4 Click more times to set additional anchor points to define the shape.

5 Click the initial anchor point to close the shape.

■ Photoshop draws a straight-sided shape.

■ Photoshop places the shape in its own layer.

Can I use the Pen to trace an object?

If the object has well-defined edges, you can trace it using the Freeform Pen tool with the Magnetic option selected in the Options bar. The tool works similarly to the Magnetic Lasso tool. For more on using the Magnetic Lasso, see Chapter 4.

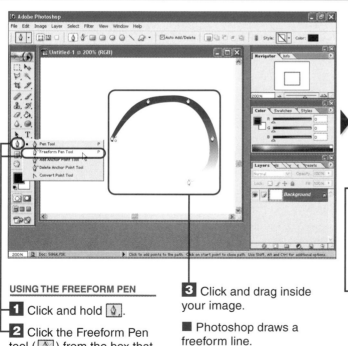

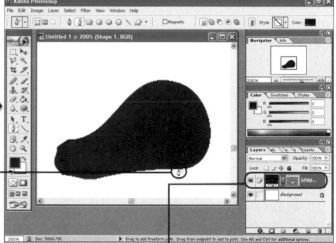

USING THE FREEFORM PEN

1 Click and hold the pen icon.

2 Click the Freeform Pen tool from the box that appears.

3 Click and drag inside your image.

■ Photoshop draws a freeform line.

4 Drag to the starting point of the line.

■ Photoshop completes the shape.

■ Alternatively, you can release the mouse, and Photoshop will complete your shape with a straight line.

■ Photoshop places the shape in its own layer.

EDIT A SHAPE

You can edit shapes by manipulating their anchor points. This lets you fine-tune the geometries of your shapes.

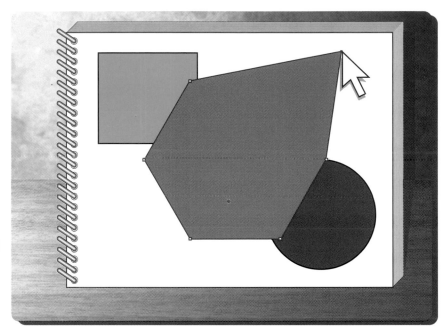

You can edit shapes drawn with Photoshop's predefined shape tools or the Pen tool.

For more shape-editing techniques, see Photoshop's Help documentation.

EDIT A SHAPE

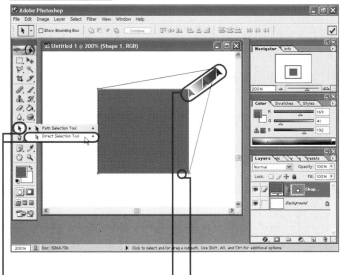 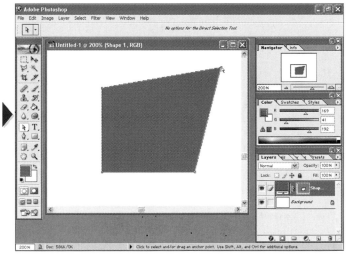

MOVE AN ANCHOR POINT

1 Click and hold the Path Selection tool (▶).

2 Click the Direct Selection tool (▶) from the box that appears.

3 Click the edge of a shape to select it.

■ Photoshop shows the anchor points that make up the shape.

4 Click and drag an anchor point.

■ Photoshop moves the anchor point, changing the geometry of the shape.

How do I edit curved lines?

If you click an anchor point situated on a curved line with the ⬧, direction lines appear to the sides of the anchor point. You can click and drag the ends of the direction lines to edit the curve on each side of the anchor point. You can also click and drag the curves themselves with the ⬧.

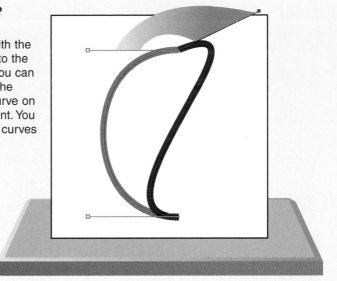

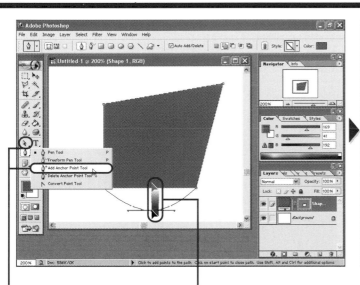

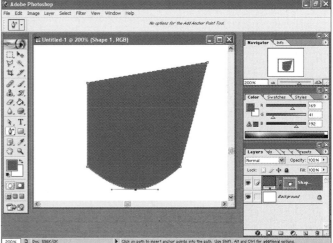

BEND A STRAIGHT SEGMENT

1 Click and hold 🖊.

2 Click the Add Anchor Point tool (🖊) from the box that appears.

3 Click a straight line between two anchor points and drag.

■ Photoshop adds an anchor point to the line.

4 Release the mouse.

■ Photoshop turns the straight line into a curved line.

■ You can use this technique to create a concave or convex curve.

CHAPTER 13

Adding and Manipulating Type

Do you want to add letters and words to your photos and illustrations? Photoshop lets you add type to your images and precisely control the type's appearance and layout. You can also stylize your type using Photoshop's filters and other tools.

ADD TYPE TO AN IMAGE

Adding type enables you to label elements in your image or use letters and words in artistic ways.

ADD TYPE TO AN IMAGE

1 Click the Type tool (T).

2 Click where you want the new type to appear.

3 Click ⊽ and select a font, style, and size for your type.

4 Click the color swatch to select a color for your type.

Note: Photoshop applies the foreground color by default. See Chapter 7 for more about selecting colors.

How do I create vertical type?

If you click and hold T, a box appears with the Vertical Type tool (IT) in it. You can use it to create up-and-down type. When using the regular Type tool, you can click the Change Orientation button (IT) to change horizontal type to vertical, and vice versa.

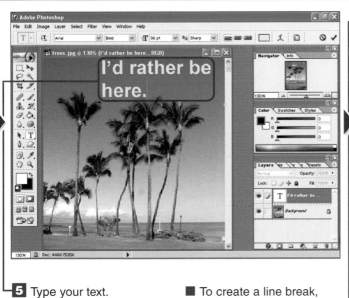

5 Type your text.

■ To create a line break, press Enter (Return).

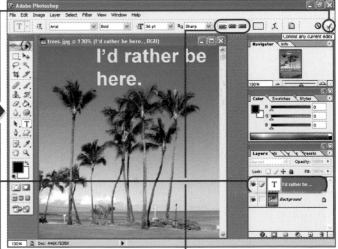

6 When you finish typing your text, click ✓ or press Enter on your keyboard's number pad.

■ Photoshop places the type in its own layer.

■ You can click the alignment buttons to left-align, center, or right-align your type.

ADD TYPE IN A BOUNDING BOX

You can add type inside a *bounding box* to constrain where the type appears and how it wraps.

ADD TYPE IN A BOUNDING BOX

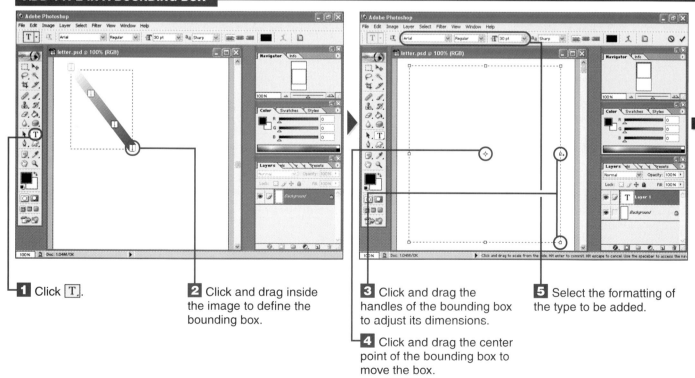

1 Click T.

2 Click and drag inside the image to define the bounding box.

3 Click and drag the handles of the bounding box to adjust its dimensions.

4 Click and drag the center point of the bounding box to move the box.

5 Select the formatting of the type to be added.

How do I format paragraph text inside a bounding box?

With T selected, click the text inside the box to highlight it. Then click **Window** and **Paragraph** to display the Paragraph palette. The palette enables you to control the alignment, indenting, and hyphenation of the text inside a bounding box. A limited selection of the palette's commands can also be performed on text that is not constrained by a bounding box.

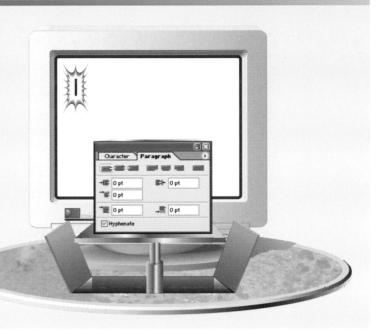

6 Type your text.

■ Your text appears inside the bounding box.

Note: When a line of text hits the edge of the bounding box, it automatically wraps to the next line. Photoshop also automatically adds hyphenation.

7 When you finish typing your text, click ✓ or press **Enter** on your keyboard's number pad.

■ The bounding box disappears.

■ To make the box reappear (in order to change its dimensions), click T and click the text.

CHANGE THE FORMATTING OF TYPE

You can change the font, style, size, and other characteristics of your type.

CHANGE THE FORMATTING OF TYPE

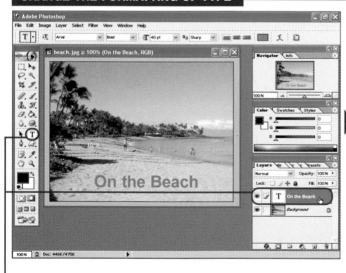

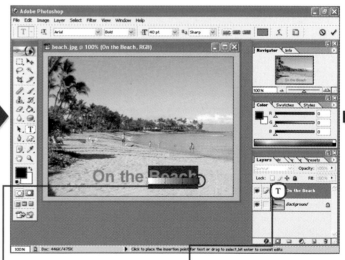

1 Click **T**.

2 Click the type layer that you want to edit.

*Note: If the Layers palette is not visible, you can click **Window** and then **Layers** to view it.*

3 Click and drag to select some type from the selected layer.

■ You can double-click the layer thumbnail to select all the type.

How do I edit the content of my type?

With the type's layer selected in the Layers palette, you can click inside the type with the T. tool. Then you can press Delete to delete letters and type to add new ones. You can press ←, →, ↑, or ↓ to move the cursor inside your type.

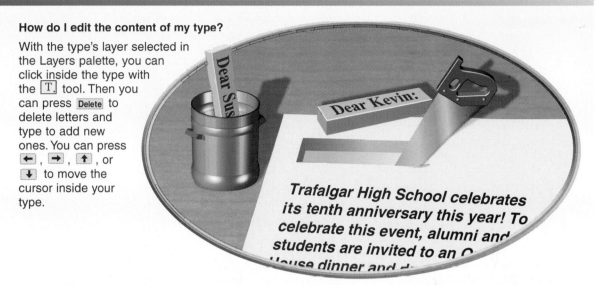

4 Click ⌄ and select a font.

5 Click ⌄ and select the type's style.

6 Click ⌄ and select the type's size.

■ You can edit your type in more complex ways by clicking **Window** and then **Character** to open the Character palette.

7 When you finish formatting your text, click ✓ or press Enter on your keyboard's number pad.

■ Photoshop applies the formatting to your type.

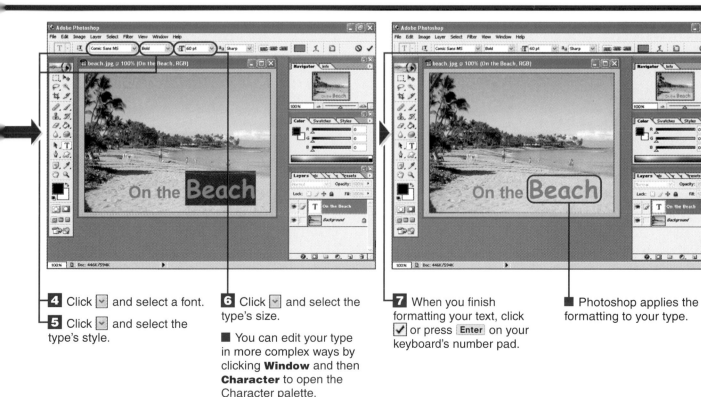

CHANGE THE COLOR OF TYPE

You can change the color of your type to make it blend or contrast with the rest of the image.

CHANGE THE COLOR OF TYPE

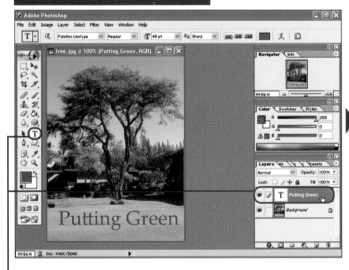

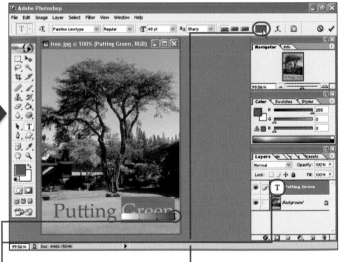

1 Click T.

2 Click the type layer that you want to edit.

*Note: If the Layers palette is not visible, you can click **Window** and then **Layers** to view it.*

3 Click and drag to select some text.

■ You can double-click the layer thumbnail to select all the type.

4 Click the Color swatch.

What is antialiasing?

Antialiasing is the process of adding semitransparent pixels to curved edges in digital images to make the edges appear more smooth. You can apply antialiasing to type to improve its appearance. Text that you do not antialias can sometimes look jagged. You can control the presence and style of your type's antialiasing with the [aa] menu in the Options bar.

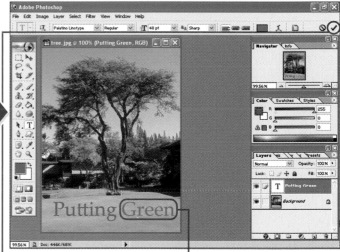

■ The Color Picker dialog box appears.

5 Click a color.

■ You can click and drag the slider (▷) to change the colors that Photoshop displays in the selection box.

6 Click **OK**.

7 Click ✓ or press **Enter** on your keyboard's number pad.

■ Photoshop changes the text to the new color.

APPLY A FILTER TO TYPE

To apply a filter to type, you must first rasterize it. Rasterizing converts your type layer into a regular Photoshop layer. You can no longer edit rasterized type using the type tools.

For more about filters, see Chapter 11.

APPLY A FILTER TO TYPE

1 Select the type layer to which you want to apply a filter.

*Note: If the Layers palette is not visible, you can click **Window** and then **Layers** to view it.*

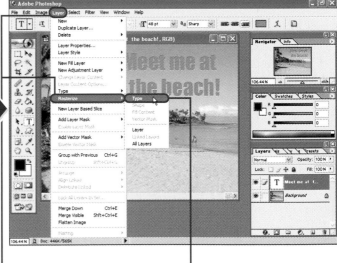

2 Click **Layer**.

3 Click **Rasterize**.

4 Click **Type**.

**How can I create
semitransparent type?**

Select the type layer in the Layers palette and then reduce the layer's opacity to less than 100%. This makes the type semitransparent. For details about changing opacity, see Chapter 9.

■ Photoshop converts the type layer to a regular layer.

■ Now you can apply a filter to the text.

■ In this example, a special effect was added to the type by clicking **Filter**, **Sketch**, and then **Bas Relief**.

APPLY AN EFFECT TO TYPE

You can easily apply an effect to type to give it a colorful or 3D appearance. After you apply an effect, you can still edit the type using the type tools.

For more about effects, see Chapter 10.

APPLY AN EFFECT TO TYPE

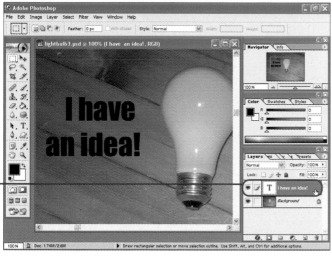

1 Select the type layer to which you want to apply an effect.

*Note: If the Layers palette is not visible, you can click **Window** and then **Layers** to view it.*

2 Click **Layer**.

3 Click **Layer Style**.

4 Click an effect.

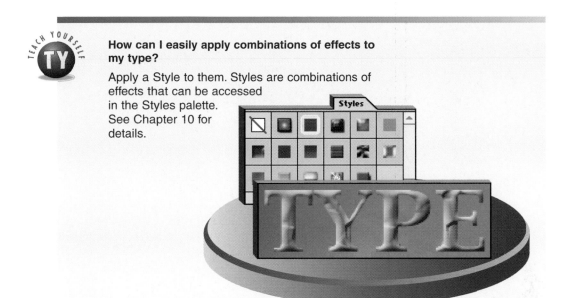

How can I easily apply combinations of effects to my type?

Apply a Style to them. Styles are combinations of effects that can be accessed in the Styles palette. See Chapter 10 for details.

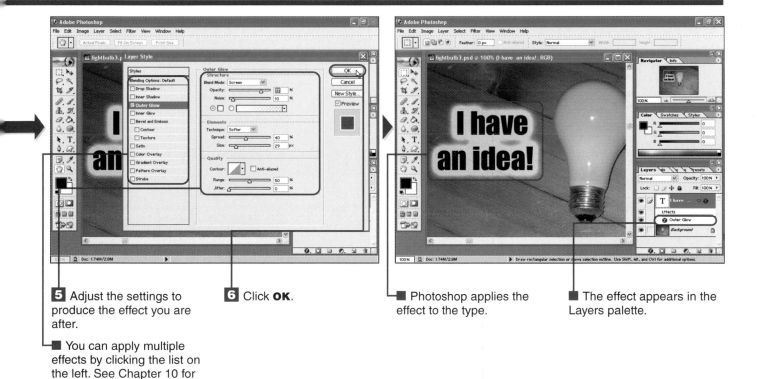

5 Adjust the settings to produce the effect you are after.

■ You can apply multiple effects by clicking the list on the left. See Chapter 10 for details.

6 Click **OK**.

■ Photoshop applies the effect to the type.

■ The effect appears in the Layers palette.

WARP TYPE

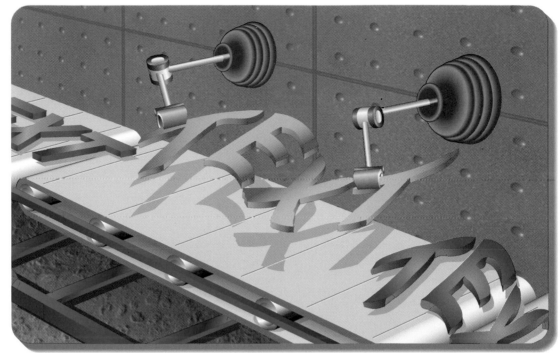

Photoshop's Warp feature lets you easily bend and distort layers of type. This can make words look wrinkled or like they are blowing in the wind.

WARP TYPE

1 Click T.

2 Click the type layer that you want to warp.

*Note: If the Layers palette is not visible, you can click **Window** and then **Layers** to view it.*

3 Click the Create Warped Text button (⬚).

■ The Warp Text dialog box appears.

4 Click the Style ⌄ (⬚).

5 Click a warp style.

How do I unwarp text?

Click the type layer that you want to unwarp and click the Create Warped Text button ([🔲]). Then click [▾] ([⬦]) and select **None** from the menu that appears. Click **OK** to unwarp the type.

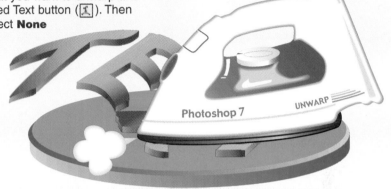

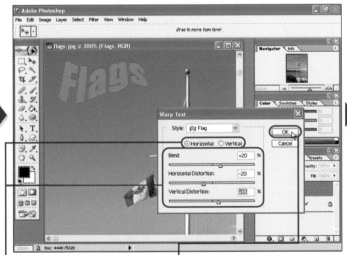

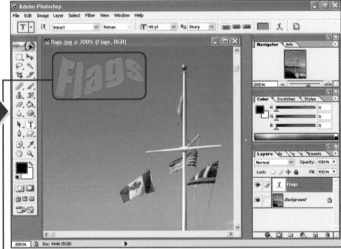

6 Select an orientation for the warp effect (○ changes to ◉).

7 Adjust the Bend and Distortion values by clicking and dragging the sliders (△).

■ The Bend and Distortion values determine the strength of the warp. At 0% for all values, no warp is applied.

8 Click **OK**.

■ Photoshop warps the text.

■ You can still edit the format, color, and other characteristics of the type after you apply warp.

Contact Sheet

Destination Folder

Reduce Size

Make CMYK

Color Range

Adjust Cyan

Blur Filter

Flatten Art

Save as EPS

CHAPTER 14

Automating Your Work

Sometimes you want to perform the same simple sequence of commands on a lot of different images. Photoshop's Action commands let you automate repetitive imaging tasks by saving sequences of commands and applying them automatically to many image files. Other Photoshop commands let you streamline your work by helping you create Web photo galleries, picture packages, and contact sheets.

RECORD AN ACTION

You can record a
sequence of commands
as an action and replay
them on other image
files. This can save you
time when you have a
task in Photoshop that
you need to repeat.

RECORD AN ACTION

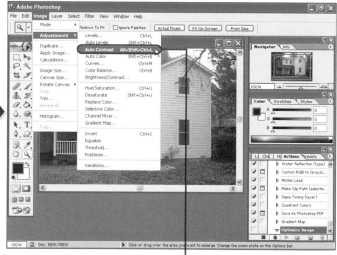

1 Click **Window**.

2 Click **Actions** to open
the Actions palette.

3 Click the Create New
Action button (🔲).

4 Type a name for your
action.

5 Click **Record**.

6 Perform the sequence of
commands that you would
like to automate on your
images.

■ In this example, the Auto
Contrast command is first
performed by clicking
Image, **Adjustments**, and
then **Auto Contrast**.

*Note: See Chapter 8 for more about
adjusting colors and contrast.*

What if I make a mistake when recording my action?

You can try recording the action again by clicking ⊙ in the Actions palette and clicking **Record Again**. This will run through the same actions and let you apply different settings in the command dialog boxes. Alternatively, you can select the action, click 🗑 to delete the action, and try rerecording it.

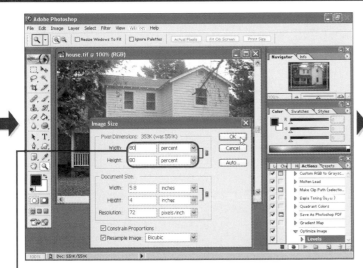

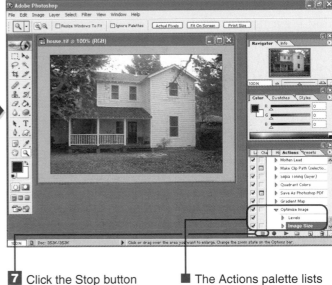

■ In this example, the image size is then reduced by 80% by clicking **Image** and **Image Size**.

Note: See Chapter 3 for more about resizing images.

7 Click the Stop button (■) to stop recording.

■ The Actions palette lists the commands performed under the name of the action.

PLAY AN ACTION

You can play an action from the Actions palette on an image. This saves time by letting you execute multiple Photoshop commands with a single click. You can also play a specific command that is part of an action by itself.

PLAY AN ACTION

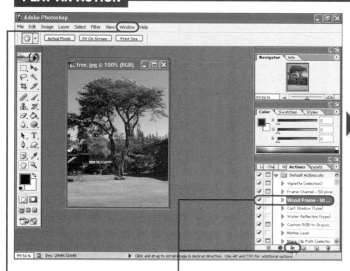

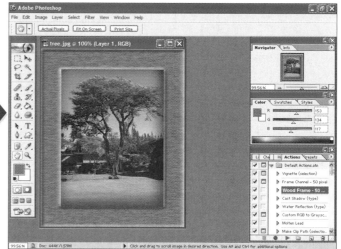

1 Click **Window** and then **Actions** to open the Actions palette.

■ Photoshop comes with a number of predefined actions in the Actions palette.

Note: To create your own action, see "Record an Action."

2 Click the action that you would like to play.

3 Click the Play button (▶).

■ Photoshop applies the commands that make up the action to the image.

■ In this example, a wood frame is added around the image.

■ You can undo the multiple commands in an action using the History palette. See Chapter 2 for more information.

How do I assign a special key command to an action?

Click 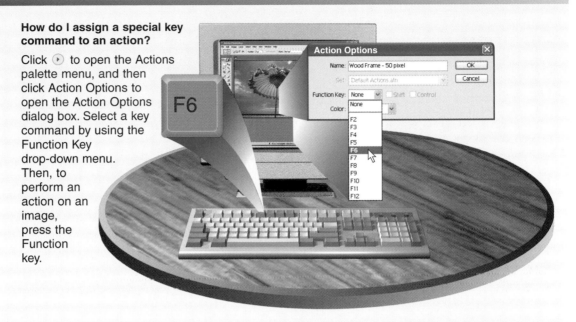 to open the Actions palette menu, and then click Action Options to open the Action Options dialog box. Select a key command by using the Function Key drop-down menu. Then, to perform an action on an image, press the Function key.

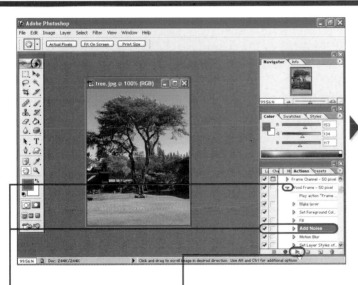

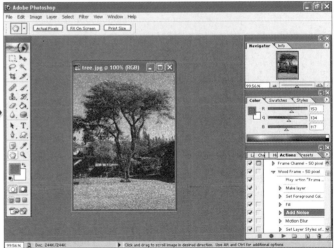

PLAY A COMMAND IN AN ACTION

1 Click ▶ to list the commands that make up an action (▶ changes to ▼).

2 Click the command that you would like to execute.

■ You can press Shift + click to select multiple commands.

3 Ctrl + click (⌘ + click) the ▶ button.

■ Photoshop executes the selected command, but no commands before or after it.

■ In this example, the selected command adds noise to the image.

BATCH PROCESS BY USING AN ACTION

You can apply an action to multiple images automatically with Photoshop's Batch command. The command is a great time-saver for tasks such as optimizing large numbers of digital photos.

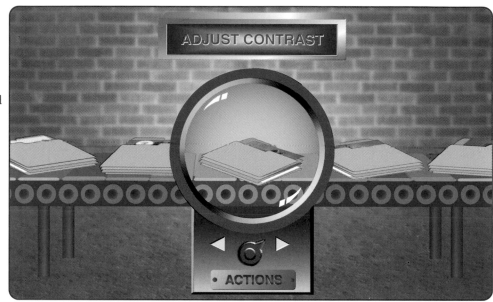

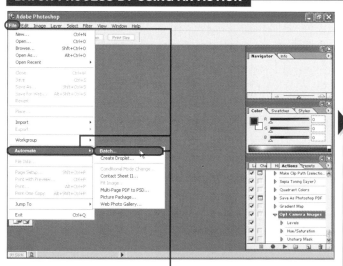

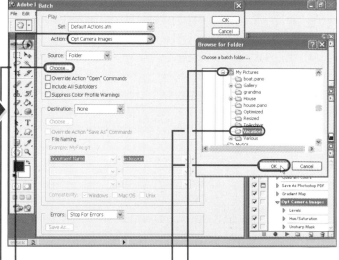

1 Place all the images you would like to apply an action to in a source folder.

2 Create a destination folder in which to save your batch-processed files.

Note: To work with folders, see your operating system's documentation.

3 Click **File**.

4 Click **Automate**.

5 Click **Batch**.

6 Click ▼ and select an action to apply.

7 Click **Choose**.

■ The Browse For Folder dialog box opens.

8 Click ➕ to open folders on your computer (➕ changes to ➖).

9 Click the folder containing your images.

10 Click **OK**.

256

How can I change the mode — such as RGB Color or Grayscale — of an image during a batch process depending on its current mode?

When you record the action, click **File**, **Automate**, and then **Conditional Mode Change**. A dialog box opens that allows you to specify the source modes that should be switched, and a target mode. When the action is run as a batch process, images that are one of the selected source modes will be converted.

How do I batch process using an action in Mac OS X?

You do this very much like a Windows user would, but with the Open dialog box instead of the Browse For Folder dialog box. Click **Choose** (step **7**), and the Open-style dialog box appears. Using the Finder-like column view in the center of the dialog box, locate the source and destination folders for your batch-processed images.

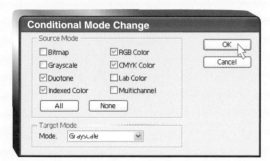

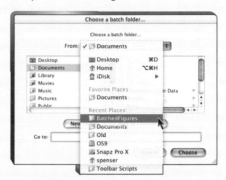

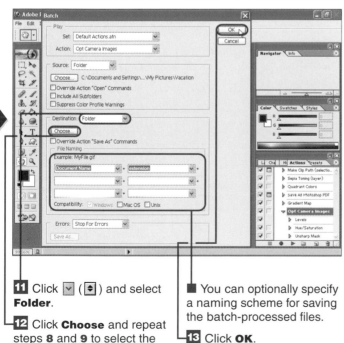

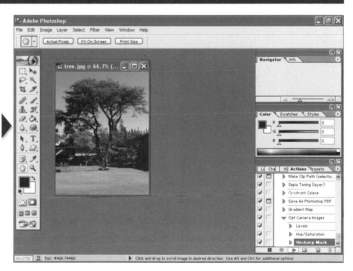

11 Click ▼ (⬍) and select **Folder**.

12 Click **Choose** and repeat steps **8** and **9** to select the folder where you would like your batch-processed files to be saved.

■ You can optionally specify a naming scheme for saving the batch-processed files.

13 Click **OK**.

■ Photoshop opens each image in the specified folder one at a time, applies the action, and then saves the files in the destination folder.

CREATE A CONTACT SHEET

Photoshop can automatically create a digital version of a photographer's contact sheet. Useful for keeping a hard-copy record of your digital images, contact sheets consist of miniature versions of images.

For information about printing a contact sheet after you have created it, see Chapter 16.

CREATE A CONTACT SHEET

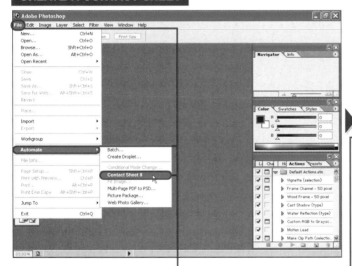

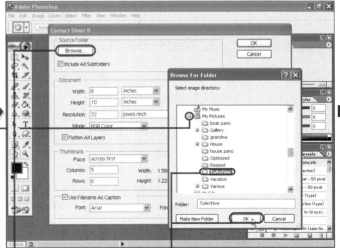

1 Place the images that you want on the contact sheet in a folder.

Note: To work with folders, see your operating system's documentation.

2 Click **File**.

3 Click **Automate**.

4 Click **Contact Sheet II**.

■ The Contact Sheet II dialog box opens.

5 Click **Browse (Choose)**.

6 In the dialog box that appears, open the folder containing your images.

■ In Windows, click ➕ to open folders on your computer (➕ changes to ➖).

■ In Mac OS 9, click the disclosure triangles to open folders.

■ In Mac OS X, use the column view in the center of the dialog box to open folders.

7 Click the folder containing your images.

8 Click **OK (Choose)**.

How do I make the thumbnail images larger on my contact sheet?

Paper size and the number of rows and columns automatically determine the size of the thumbnails. To change the thumbnail size, type the number of rows and columns you want on the sheet in the Columns and Rows boxes in the Contact Sheet II dialog box.

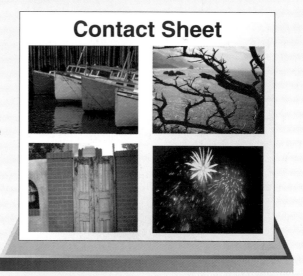

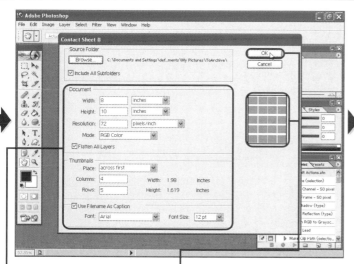

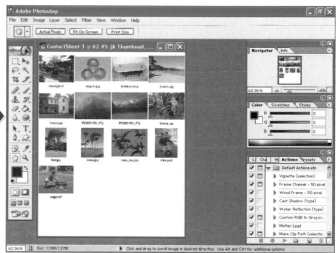

9 Set any contact sheet properties by typing values or by clicking ⌄ (⬍) and selecting settings.

■ You can set the contact sheet size and resolution, the order and number of columns and rows in the sheet as well as the caption font and font size.

■ Photoshop displays a preview of the layout.

10 Click **OK**.

■ Photoshop creates and displays your contact sheet.

■ If there are more images than can fit on a single page, Photoshop creates multiple contact sheets.

CREATE A PICTURE PACKAGE

You can automatically create a one-page layout with a selected image at various sizes using the Picture Package command. You may find this useful when you want to print pictures for friends, family, or associates.

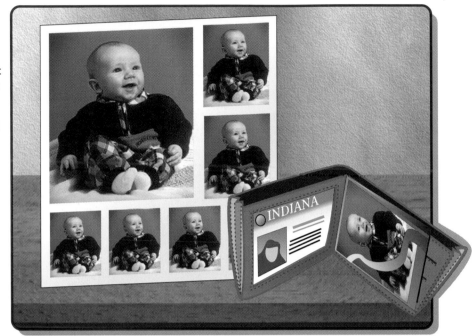

For information about printing a picture package after you have created it, see Chapter 16.

CREATE A PICTURE PACKAGE

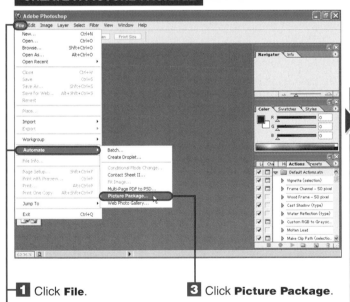

1 Click **File**.

2 Click **Automate**.

3 Click **Picture Package**.

■ The Picture Package dialog box opens.

4 Click **Browse** (**Choose**).

■ The Select an Image File dialog box opens.

5 Select the folder that contains the image file.

■ In Windows, click ⌄ and select the folder that contains the image file.

■ In either Mac OS, use the Open-style dialog box to navigate to the folder containing the image file.

6 Click the image file.

7 Click **Open**.

How do I label my picture package?

At the bottom of the Picture Package dialog box, you can choose labels such as copyright or caption information, the image filename, or custom text that you define. To set copyright and caption information for an image, see Chapter 15.

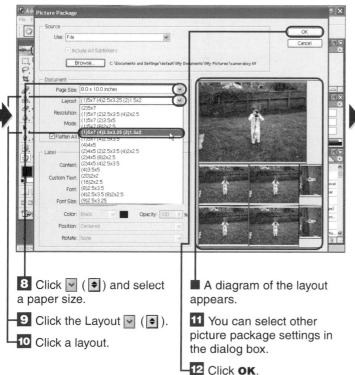

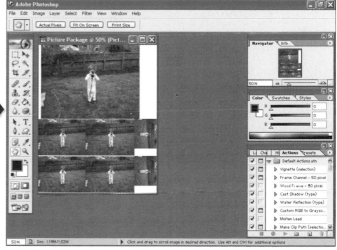

■ **8** Click ☑ (⬍) and select a paper size.

■ **9** Click the Layout ☑ (⬍).

■ **10** Click a layout.

■ A diagram of the layout appears.

11 You can select other picture package settings in the dialog box.

12 Click **OK**.

■ Photoshop constructs the picture package step-by-step, then opens a new image window with the picture package inside it.

CREATE A WEB PHOTO GALLERY

You can have Photoshop create a photo gallery Web site that showcases your images. Photoshop not only sizes and optimizes your image files for the site, but it also creates the Web pages that display the images and links those pages together.

After you create your photo gallery, you can use a Web publishing program such as Macromedia Dreamweaver or Adobe Go Live to upload your images to a Web server.

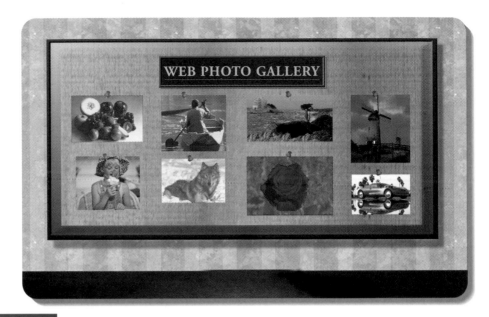

CREATE A WEB PHOTO GALLERY

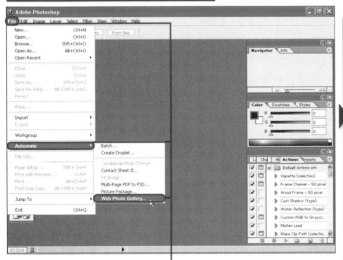

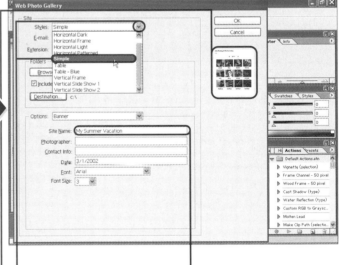

1 Place all the images you would like to feature in your Web photo gallery in a folder.

2 Create a separate folder where Photoshop can save all the image files and HTML files necessary for your gallery.

Note: To work with folders, see your operating system's documentation.

3 Click **File**.

4 Click **Automate**.

5 Click **Web Photo Gallery**.

6 Click ☑ (⧉) and select a photo gallery style.

■ Photoshop displays a preview of the style.

7 Type the site name information for your gallery Web pages.

How can I customize the pages in my Web photo galleries?

You can customize your pages by selecting different gallery styles in the Web Photo Gallery dialog box. The different styles organize the text and images in different ways on the Web pages. Some of the styles organize the gallery content into a framed Web site. You can also select different settings from the Options list to customize image sizes and link colors for the gallery.

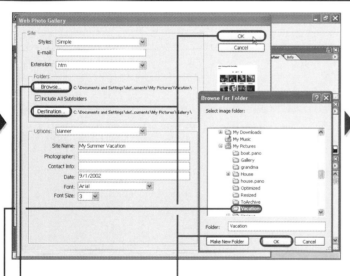

8 Click **Browse** (**Choose**).

9 In the dialog box that appears, select the folder containing your images.

■ In Windows, select the folder from the Browse For Folder dialog box.

■ In either Mac OS, use the Open-style dialog box to navigate to the folder containing the image file.

10 Click **OK** (**Choose**).

11 Click **Destination** and repeat steps **9** and **10** to specify the folder in which to save your gallery.

12 Click **OK** in the Web Photo Gallery dialog box.

■ Photoshop opens each image in the specified folder, creates versions for the photo gallery, and generates the necessary HTML code.

■ After the processing is complete, Photoshop opens the default Web browser on your computer and displays the home page of the gallery.

■ You can click a thumbnail to see a larger version of the image.

CHAPTER 15

Saving Images

Do you want to save your images for use later? Or so that you can use them in another application or on the Web? This chapter shows you how.

SAVE IN THE PHOTOSHOP FORMAT

You can save your image in Photoshop's native image format. This format enables you to retain multiple layers in your image, if it has them. This is the best format in which to save your images if you still need to edit them.

The Photoshop PDF and TIFF file formats also support multiple layers.

SAVE IN THE PHOTOSHOP FORMAT

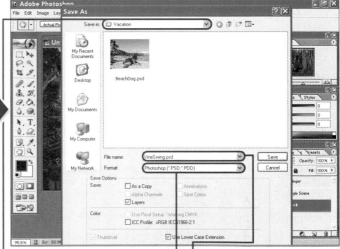

1 Click **File**.

2 Click **Save As**.

■ If you have named and saved your image previously and just want to save changes, you can click **File** and then **Save**.

■ The Save As dialog box appears.

3 Click ▼ (◆) and click a folder in which to save the image file.

4 Click ▼ (◆) and select the Photoshop file format.

5 Type a name for the image file.

■ Photoshop automatically assigns a .psd extension.

How do I choose a file format for my image?

You should choose the format based on how you want to use the image. If it is a multilayered image and you want to preserve the layers, save it as a Photoshop file. If you want to use it in word processing or page layout applications, save it as a TIFF or EPS file. If you want to use it on the Web, save it as a JPEG or GIF file. For more information on file formats, see the rest of this chapter as well as Photoshop's documentation.

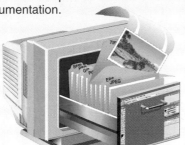

How do I save in the Photoshop format with Mac OS X?

You start by clicking **File**, then **Save As**. The Save As dialog box appears. Navigate to where you want to save the file by clicking the Show More button (■) to display the column browser, or by clicking the Where (■) and choosing from recent and Favorite folders. Click the Format (■) and choose **Photoshop**; Photoshop adds the .psd file extension.

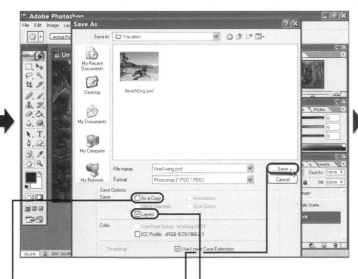

■ If you want to save a copy of the file and keep the existing file open, click **As a Copy** (☐ changes to ☑).

■ If you want to merge the multiple layers of your image into one layer, click **Layers** (☑ changes to ☐).

6 Click **Save**.

■ Photoshop saves the image file.

■ The name of the file appears in the image's title bar.

SAVE AN IMAGE FOR USE IN ANOTHER APPLICATION

You can save your image in a format that users can open and use in other imaging or page-layout applications. TIFF (Tagged Image File Format) and EPS (Encapsulated PostScript) are standard printing formats that many applications on both Windows and Macintosh platforms support.

BMP — bitmap — is a popular Windows image format, and PICT is a popular Macintosh image format.

Most image formats — with the exception of the Photoshop PSD, Photoshop PDF, and TIFF formats — do not support layers.

SAVE AN IMAGE FOR USE IN ANOTHER APPLICATION

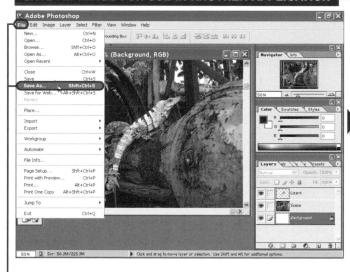

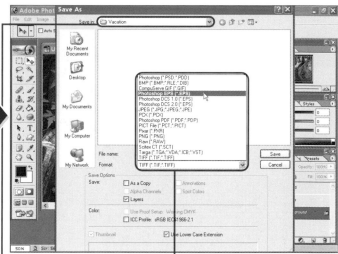

1 Click **File**.

2 Click **Save As**.

■ The Save As dialog box appears.

3 Choose a folder in which to save the image file.

■ Click ☑ (⬍) and choose a folder.

■ In Mac OS X, click the Where ⬍ to choose a recent or Favorite folder, or click ⬍ to display a column browser to navigate to the desired folder.

4 Click ☑ (⬍) and select a file format.

What are some popular page-layout programs with which I might use images?

Adobe PageMaker, Adobe InDesign, and QuarkXPress are three popular page-layout programs. They let you combine text and images to create brochures, magazines, and other printed media. You can import TIFF and EPS files saved in Photoshop into all three programs.

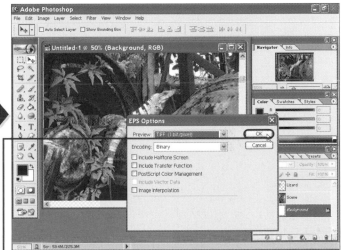

■ If you are saving a multilayer image and select a file format that does not support layers, an alert icon appears. Photoshop will save a flattened copy of the image.

Note: See "Save in the Photoshop Format" to save a multilayer image. For more about flattening, see Chapter 9.

5 Type a filename.

■ Photoshop assigns an appropriate extension for the file format, such as `.tif` or `.eps`.

6 Click **Save**.

■ When saving in the EPS format, as in this example, Photoshop displays a dialog box allowing you to specify optional settings. Click **OK**.

■ Photoshop saves the image.

■ If a flattened copy was saved, the original multilayer version remains in the image window.

SAVE A JPEG FOR THE WEB

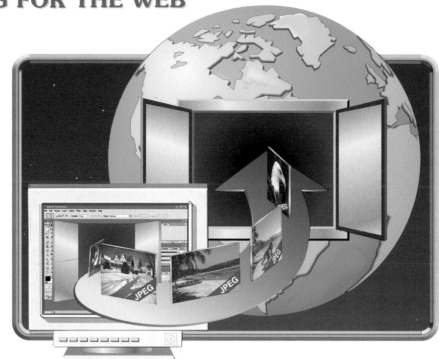

You can save a file in the JPEG — Joint Photographic Experts Group — format and publish it on the Web. JPEG is the preferred Web file format for saving photographic images.

JPEG images are always saved at a resolution of 72 dpi.

SAVE A JPEG FOR THE WEB

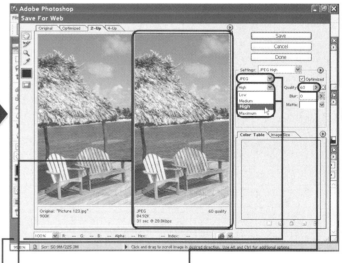

1 Click **File**.

2 Click **Save for Web**.

■ The Save For Web dialog box appears.

3 Click the right preview window.

4 Click ☑ (◘) and select **JPEG**.

5 Click ☑ (◘) and select a quality setting.

■ Alternatively, you can select a numeric quality setting from 0, low quality, to 100, high quality.

■ The higher the quality, the larger the resulting file size.

What is image compression?

Image compression involves using mathematical techniques to reduce the amount of information required to describe an image. This results in small file sizes, which is important when transmitting information on the Internet. Some compression schemes, such as JPEG, involve some loss in quality due to the compression, but the loss is usually negligible compared to the file size savings.

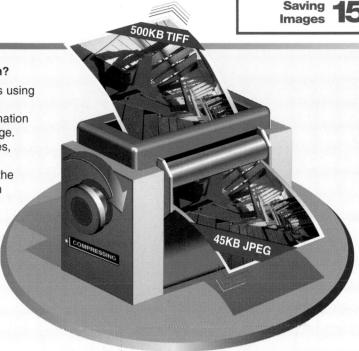

■6 Check that the file quality and size are acceptable in the preview window.

■ You can use 🖑 to move the image in the preview window.

■ You can use 🔍 to magnify the image in the preview window.

■7 Click **Save**.

■8 Select a folder in which to save the file.

■ Click ⬇ (⬍) and select a folder.

■ In Mac OS X, navigate by clicking the Where ⬍ or ⬇ to display the column browser.

■9 Type in a filename. A `.jpg` extension is assigned.

■10 Click **Save**.

■ Photoshop saves the JPEG file in an "images" subfolder in the selected folder.

■ The original image file remains open in Photoshop.

SAVE A GIF FOR THE WEB

You can save a file as a *GIF* — Graphics Interchange Format — and publish it on the Web. The GIF format is good for saving illustrations that have a lot of solid color. The format supports a maximum of 256 colors.

GIF images are always saved at a resolution of 72 dpi.

SAVE A GIF FOR THE WEB

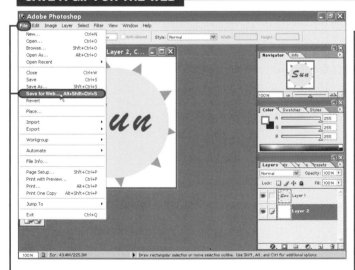

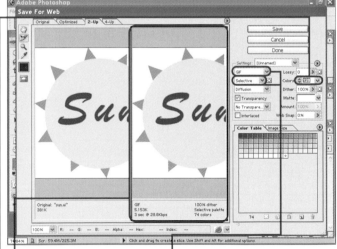

1 Click **File**.

2 Click **Save for Web**.

■ The Save For Web dialog box appears.

3 Click the right preview window.

4 Click ⬇ (⬍) and select **GIF**.

5 Click ⬍ and select the number of colors to include in the image.

■ GIF allows a maximum of 256 colors, making it unsuitable for most photos.

■ You can click ⬇ (⬍) to choose the palette from which Photoshop selects the GIF colors.

How do I minimize the file sizes of my GIF images?

The most important factor in creating small GIFs is limiting the number of colors in the final image. GIF files are limited to 256 colors or fewer. In images that have just a few solid colors, you can often reduce the total number of colors to 16 or 8 without any noticeable reduction in quality. See step **5** below for setting the number of colors in your GIF images.

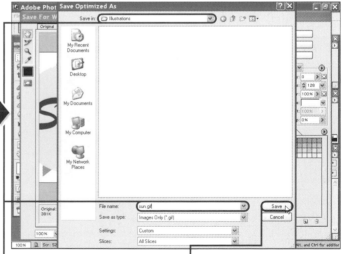

6 Check that the file quality and size are acceptable in the preview window.

■ You can use 🖑 to move the image in the preview window.

■ You can use 🔍 to magnify the image in the preview window.

7 Click **Save**.

8 Select a folder in which to save the file.

■ Click ⬇ (⬍) and select a folder.

■ In Mac OS X, navigate by clicking the Where ⬍ or ⬇ to display the column browser.

9 Type a filename. A `.gif` extension is assigned.

10 Click **Save**.

■ Photoshop saves the GIF file in an "images" subfolder in the selected folder.

■ The original image file remains open in Photoshop.

SAVE A GIF WITH TRANSPARENCY

You can include transparency in files saved in the GIF file format. The transparent pixels do not show up on Web pages.

Because Photoshop background layers cannot contain transparent pixels, you need to work with non-background layers to create transparent GIFs. See Chapter 9 for more about layers.

SAVE A GIF WITH TRANSPARENCY

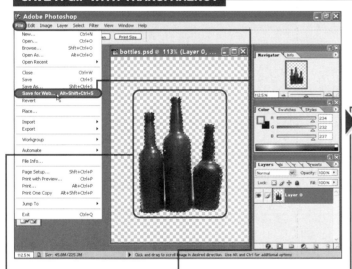

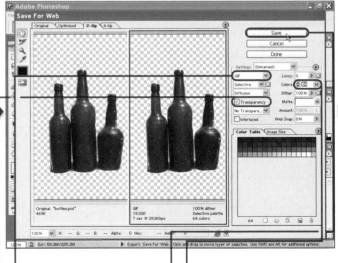

1 Select the area that you want to make transparent with a selection tool.

Note: See Chapter 4 for more on using selection tools.

2 Press Delete to delete the pixels.

■ Photoshop replaces the deleted pixels with a checkerboard pattern.

3 Click **File**.

4 Click **Save for Web**.

5 Click ⯆ (⬍) and select **GIF**.

6 Click **Transparency** to retain transparency in the saved file (☐ changes to ☑).

7 Click ⬍ and select the number of colors to include in the image.

■ GIF allows a maximum of 256 colors.

8 Click **Save**.

9 Select a folder in which to save the file.

274

**Does the JPEG format
support transparency?**

No. JPEG, the other
popular image format
for the Web, does not
support transparency.
However, you can
simulate transparency
in a JPEG image by
surrounding elements
in the image with a
color that matches the
intended background.

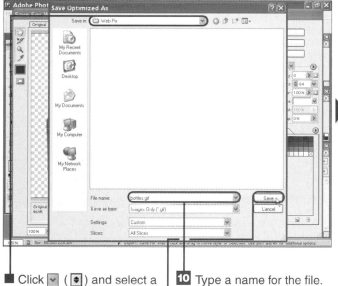

■ Click ☑ (🖢) and select a
folder.

■ In Mac OS X, navigate by
clicking the Where 🖢 or ☑
to display the column
browser.

10 Type a name for the file.

■ Photoshop automatically
assigns a `.gif` extension.

11 Click **Save**.

■ In this example, the image
has been added to a Web
page and opened in a Web
browser.

■ The transparency causes
the Web page background to
show through around the
edges of the object.

SAVE A GIF WITH WEB-SAFE COLORS

You can save your GIF images using only Web-safe colors. This ensures that the images appear the way you expect in browsers running on 256-color monitors.

You can create Web-safe images only in the GIF format.

SAVE A GIF WITH WEB-SAFE COLORS

1 Click **File**.

2 Click **Save for Web**.

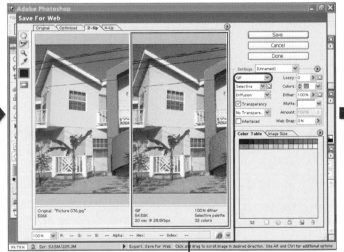

■ The Save For Web dialog box appears.

3 Click ⏷ (⬍) and select **GIF**.

Should I save all my Web images with Web-safe colors?

Not necessarily. Nowadays, most people surf the Web on monitors set to thousands of colors or more, which makes Web safety less relevant. Also, it is often better to save photographic Web images as non-Web-safe JPEGs because the GIF file format offers poor compression and quality when it comes to photos.

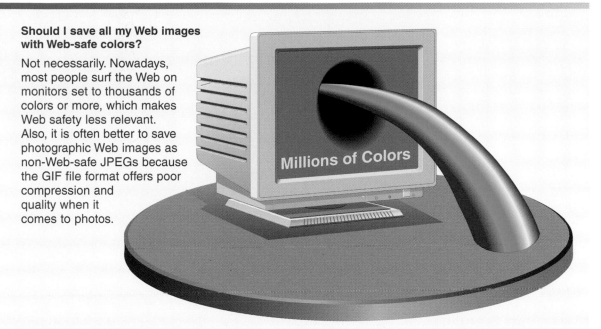

Millions of Colors

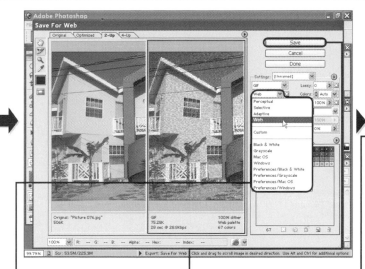

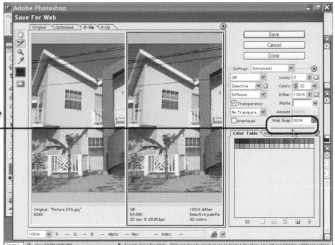

4 Click ▼ (◆) and select **Web** as the color palette type.

Note: When you do not specify Web-safe colors, Photoshop saves the image by choosing from all the colors available in the spectrum.

■ Photoshop now uses only colors from the palette available to browsers running on 256-color monitors.

5 Click **Save** to save the image.

MAKE A GIF PARTIALLY WEB SAFE

■ You can specify a degree of Web safety from 1% to 100% using the Web Snap menu.

Note: The Web Snap menu lets you find a compromise between creating a totally Web-safe image — which may display poorly — and an image that has colors from the entire spectrum.

COMPARE FILE SIZES

You can compare the results of different compression schemes on your Web images. This helps you choose which scheme is most efficient and generates the best-looking image at a reasonable file size. You can then save the image using that scheme.

COMPARE FILE SIZES

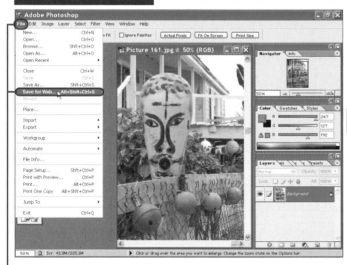

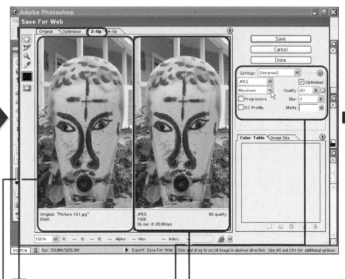

1 Click **File**.

2 Click **Save for Web**.

■ The Save For Web dialog box opens.

3 Click **2-Up**.

■ Photoshop displays the original image on the left side.

■ Photoshop displays the image with the optimized settings applied on the right side.

4 To select different settings, click either image and change the settings in the right side of the dialog box.

What file size should I make my Web images?

If a large portion of your audience uses dial-up modems to view your Web pages, keep your images small enough so that total page size — which includes all the images on the page plus the HTML file — is below 50K. You can check the file size and the download speed of an image at the bottom of the Save For Web preview pane. To change an image's file size and download speed, you can adjust the quality and color settings in the Save For Web dialog box. See "Save a JPEG for the Web" and "Save a GIF for the Web" for details.

■ Photoshop displays the image with the new settings applied.

■ The new file size is displayed.

5 Click **4-Up** to compare four versions of the image at a time.

■ Photoshop displays four versions of the image.

■ You can change the speed that Photoshop uses to estimate the download time by clicking the top menu ⊙ and selecting an option.

ADD CAPTION, COPYRIGHT, AND KEYWORD INFORMATION

You can store caption and copyright information with your saved image. You may find this useful if you plan on publishing the images online.

Some image editing applications — such as Photoshop — can detect copyright information from an image and display it to a user who opens it.

ADD CAPTION AND COPYRIGHT INFORMATION

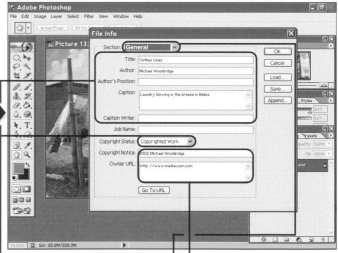

1 Click **File**.

2 Click **File Info**.

■ The File Info dialog box appears.

3 Type caption and author information for the image.

4 Click ⊡ (⊟) and select a Copyright Status.

5 Type the copyright information for the image.

6 Click ⊡ (⊟) and select Keywords.

How do I retrieve information about a photo taken with a digital camera?

Information about photos taken with a digital camera is stored as EXIF information. You can view it in the Caption dialog box by clicking the Section ☑ (🖶) and selecting **EXIF**. This information includes the make and model of the camera and the date and time the photo was shot.

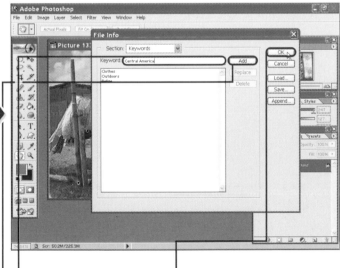

7 Type a keyword for the image.

8 Click **Add**.

■ Photoshop adds the keyword.

9 Repeat steps **7** and **8** for each keyword.

10 Click **OK**.

■ Photoshop places a copyright symbol in the title bar.

■ To save the copyrighted image, see the other tasks in this chapter.

SAVE A SLICED IMAGE

You can save an image that has been sliced with the Slice tool. Photoshop saves the slices as different images and also saves an HTML file that organizes the slices into a Web page. Slices enable you to save some parts of an image as GIF and others as JPEG. This can result in an overall image that has a smaller file size.

For more information about using the Slice tool, see Chapter 4.

SAVE A SLICED IMAGE

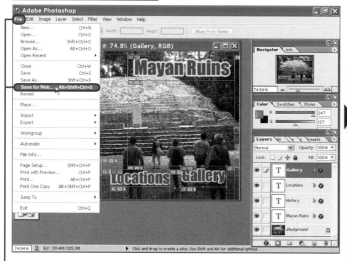

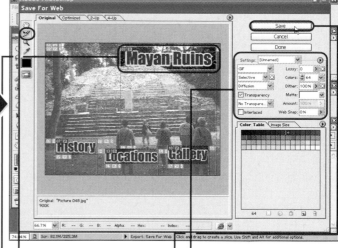

1 Open your sliced image.

2 Click **File**.

3 Click **Save for Web**.

■ The Save For Web dialog box opens.

4 Click the Slice Select tool ().

5 Click one of the image slices to select it.

6 Specify the optimization settings for the slice.

7 Repeat steps **5** and **6** for each of the slices.

8 Click **Save**.

9 Select a folder in which to save the file.

How do I publish my Web page online?

After you have created a Web page by saving your sliced Photoshop image, you can make the page available online by transferring the HTML and image files to a Web server. Most people arrange for Web server access through an Internet service provider (ISP).

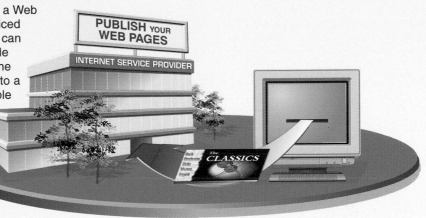

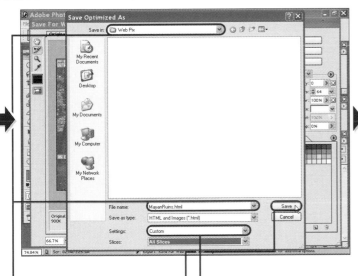

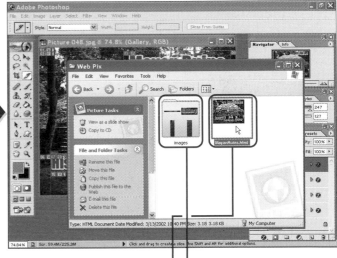

■ Click ☑ (⬍) and select a folder.

■ In Mac OS X, navigate by clicking the Where ⬍ or ⬍ to display the column browser.

10 Type a name for the file.

■ Photoshop saves the images by appending slice numbers to the original image name. To change the naming scheme, you can click the Settings ☑ (⬍) and click **Other**.

11 Click **Save** to save the files.

■ You can access the HTML and image files in the folder that was specified.

■ The image files are saved in a separate images subfolder.

12 To view the Web page, double-click the HTML file.

CHAPTER 16

PREVIEW

Printing Images

Printing enables you to save the digital imagery you create in Photoshop in hard-copy form. Photoshop can print to black-and-white or color printers.

PRINT ON A PC

You can print your
Photoshop image in
color or black-and-
white on a PC using
an ink-jet, laser, or
other type of printer.

PRINT ON A PC

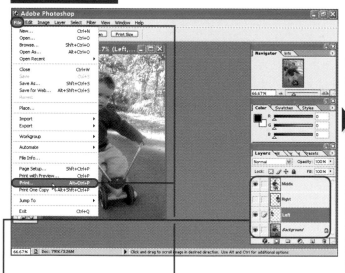

1 Make sure that the layers
you want to print are visible.

*Note: An 👁 means that a layer is
visible. To learn more about layers,
see Chapter 9.*

2 Click **File**.

3 Click **Print**.

■ If your image is larger
than your printer paper, a
warning appears. Click
Proceed.

■ The Print dialog box
appears.

4 Click 🔽 and select a
printer to use.

5 Click 🔼 to select the
number of copies.

6 Click **Properties**.

Is there a shortcut for quickly printing one copy of an image?

To print your image on the currently selected printer using the current print settings, click **File** and then **Print One Copy**. This will skip the Print and Document Properties dialog boxes.

PRINT
ONE COPY

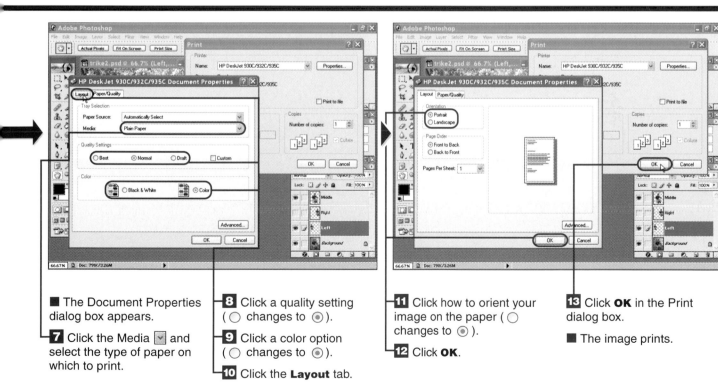

■ The Document Properties dialog box appears.

7 Click the Media ⌄ and select the type of paper on which to print.

8 Click a quality setting (○ changes to ◉).

9 Click a color option (○ changes to ◉).

10 Click the **Layout** tab.

11 Click how to orient your image on the paper (○ changes to ◉).

12 Click **OK**.

13 Click **OK** in the Print dialog box.

■ The image prints.

You can print your Photoshop image in color or black-and-white on a Macintosh using an ink-jet, laser, or other type of printer.

PRINT ON A MACINTOSH

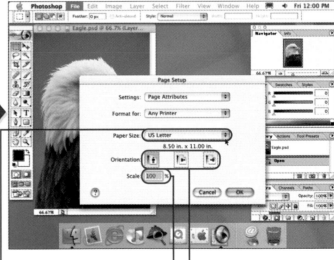

SET UP THE PAGE

1 Make sure that the layers you want to print are visible.

Note: An 👁 means that a layer is visible. To learn more about layers, see Chapter 9.

2 Click **File**.

3 Click **Page Setup**.

■ The Page Setup dialog box appears.

4 Click 🔲 and select a paper size.

5 Choose an orientation: .

■ You can type a value in the Scale text box to increase or decrease the printed size on the page.

What is halftoning?

In grayscale printing, halftoning is the process by which a printer creates the appearance of different shades of gray using only black ink. If you look closely at a grayscale image printed on most black-and-white laser printers, you see that the image consists of tiny, differently sized dot patterns. Larger dots produce the darker gray areas of the image while smaller dots produce the lighter gray areas.

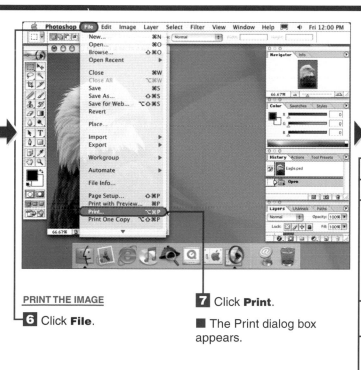

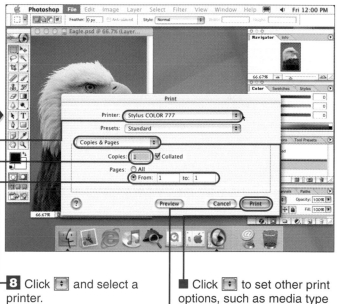

PRINT THE IMAGE

6 Click **File**.

7 Click **Print**.

■ The Print dialog box appears.

8 Click 🔽 and select a printer.

9 Type the number of copies to print.

10 Click the range of pages you want to print (◯ changes to ◉) and type a range, if necessary.

■ Click 🔽 to set other print options, such as media type and layout, specific to the printer chosen.

11 Click **Print**.

■ The image prints.

PREVIEW A PRINTOUT

PREVIEW

Photoshop lets you preview your printout, as well as adjust the size and positioning of your printed image, in a special dialog box. Previewing lets you check and adjust your work before putting ink on paper.

PREVIEW A PRINTOUT

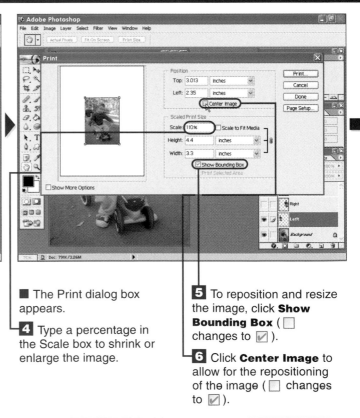

1 Make sure that the layers you want to print are visible.

Note: An [icon] means that a layer is visible. To learn more about layers, see Chapter 9.

2 Click **File**.

3 Click **Print with Preview**.

■ The Print dialog box appears.

4 Type a percentage in the Scale box to shrink or enlarge the image.

5 To reposition and resize the image, click **Show Bounding Box** (☐ changes to ☑).

6 Click **Center Image** to allow for the repositioning of the image (☐ changes to ☑).

How can I maximize the size of my image on the printed page?

In the Print Preview dialog box, you can click **Scale to Fit Media** (☐ changes to ☑) to scale the image to the maximum size given the current printing settings.

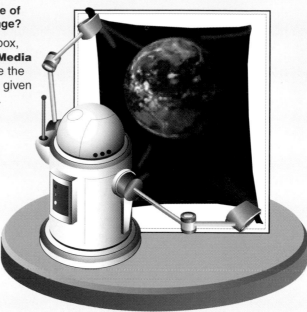

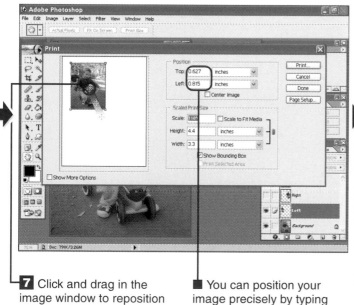

7 Click and drag in the image window to reposition the image on the page.

■ You can position your image precisely by typing values in the Top and Left fields.

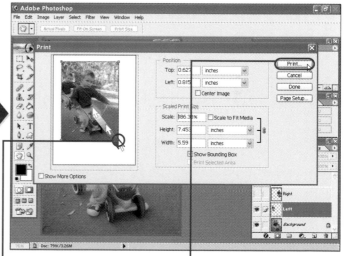

8 Click and drag the handles on the image corners to scale the image by hand.

9 To print the image, click **Print**.

CHAPTER 17

Performance Tips

Photoshop is notorious for using up lots of computer memory. This chapter gives you some tips on making sure that the application has enough memory to run at top speed. It also shows you how to ensure that Photoshop uses what memory it is given efficiently.

You can give Photoshop extra memory — known as *scratch disk space* — from your hard drive to use when it runs out of RAM, or random access memory. This enables you to open up more files at once.

will work for memory

ALLOCATE SCRATCH DISK SPACE

1 Click **Edit** (**Photoshop**, Mac OS X).

2 Click **Preferences**.

3 Click **Plug-Ins & Scratch Disks**.

■ The Preferences dialog box appears.

■ Photoshop uses your startup drive for scratch space by default.

■ If you have more than one hard drive available, you can click ☑ (⬍) and specify that Photoshop use other drives when it needs to.

Note: You can specify up to four drives, total.

4 Click **OK**.

How do I allocate more RAM to Photoshop?

On a PC or a Macintosh running OS 9, click **Edit** (**Photoshop**, Mac OS X), **Preferences**, and then **Memory & Image Cache**. To boost the RAM allocated to Photoshop, increase the Used By Photoshop value. On a Macintosh running Mac OS 9 or earlier, you can also select the Photoshop application icon in the Finder and then click **File**, **Get Info**, and **Memory**. You can set the minimum and preferred memory sizes in the dialog box that appears.

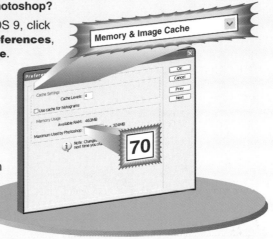

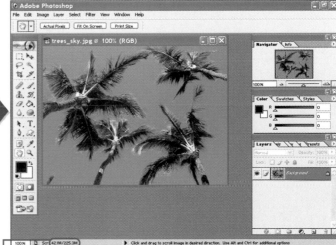

CHECK AVAILABLE MEMORY

1 Click ▶.

2 Click **Scratch Sizes**.

■ The left number is the amount of memory being used by Photoshop. The right number is the total amount of RAM available.

Note: If the left number is greater than the right, Photoshop is using scratch disk space.

LUSING THE PURGE COMMAND

You can free up the RAM that Photoshop uses to remember past commands so that it can use this memory for other purposes. This can boost Photoshop's speed.

USING THE PURGE COMMAND

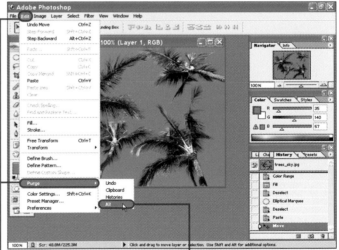

■ Photoshop displays previously executed commands in the History palette. Each command represents information stored in your computer's memory.

■ If the History palette is hidden, you can click **Window** and then **History** to display it.

1 Click **Edit**.

2 Click **Purge**.

■ You can click **Undo** to purge the previous command, **Clipboard** to purge information stored from a cut or copy command, or **Histories** to purge commands stored in the History palette.

3 To purge all the information, click **All**.

Note: Do not use the Purge commands if you need to use any of Photoshop's stored information.

Why can freeing up memory cause Photoshop to run faster?

When all the available fast memory — RAM — in your computer is used up, Photoshop starts storing information in your computer's hard drive memory. This memory is much slower. Consequently, purging Photoshop's memory and keeping as much RAM free as possible can keep the program running at top speed.

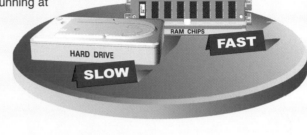

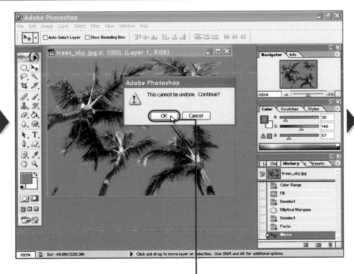

■ Photoshop displays a warning.

4 Click **OK**.

■ Photoshop purges the information from its memory

■ Photoshop deletes all the commands but the most recent one from the History palette.

ADJUST HISTORY SETTINGS

You can control the amount of information stored in the History palette. This enables you to keep that information from taking up too much memory and slowing down Photoshop.

ADJUST HISTORY SETTINGS

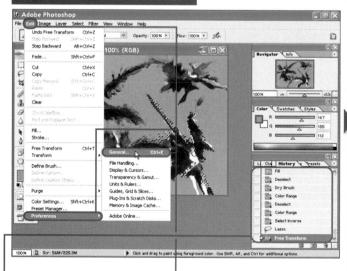

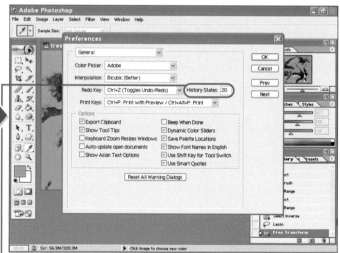

■ Photoshop displays previously executed commands in the History palette.

■ If the History palette is hidden, you can click **Window** and then **History** to display it.

1 Click **Edit** (**Photoshop**, Mac OS X).

2 Click **Preferences**.

3 Click **General**.

■ The Preferences dialog box appears.

■ The History States value is the maximum number of commands Photoshop will remember at a time.

Note: To find out how to use the History palette to undo commands, see Chapter 2.

How much RAM — random access memory — does Photoshop need to run efficiently?

When it comes to running Photoshop efficiently, you can never have enough RAM. Multilayered files can take up many megabytes of memory when you have them opened. Photoshop also uses RAM for every command it stores in its history. You need a minimum of 128MB of RAM to run Photoshop, but it is a good idea to have twice that, especially if you are working with large files that have a lot of layers. You need at least 280MB of hard drive space to install Photoshop.

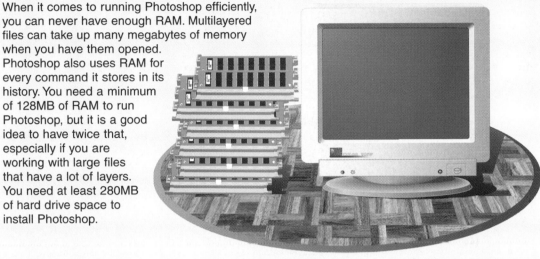

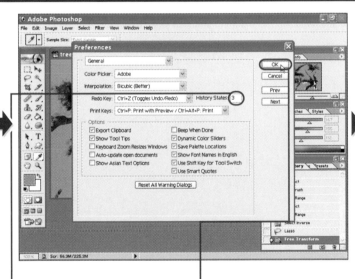

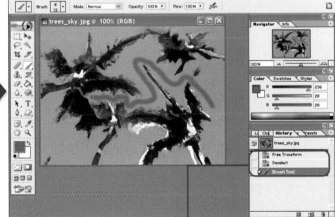

4 Type a lower number to reduce the amount of memory the History palette uses.

5 Click **OK**.

6 Perform a command.

Note: In this example, the paintbrush was used.

■ Photoshop deletes older History commands it had saved.

INDEX

INDEX

INDEX